The Faerie Queene by

Book II. The Legend of Sir Guyon

THE SECOND BOOKE OF THE FAERIE QUEENE CONTAYNING THE LEGEND OF SIR GUYON OR OF TEMPERAUNCE

One of the greatest of English poets, Edmund Spenser was born in East Smithfield, London, in 1552. He was educated in London at the Merchant Taylors' School and later at Pembroke College, Cambridge. In 1579, he published The Shepheardes Calender, his first major work.

Edmund journeyed to Ireland in July 1580, in the service of the newly appointed Lord Deputy, Arthur Grey, 14th Baron Grey de Wilton. His time included the terrible massacre at the Siege of Smerwick.

The epic poem, The Faerie Queene, is acknowledged as Edmund's masterpiece. The first three books were published in 1590, and a second set of three books were published in 1596.

Indeed the reality is that Spenser, through his great talents, was able to move Poetry in a different direction. It led to him being called a Poet's Poet and brought rich admiration from Milton, Raleigh, Blake, Wordsworth, Keats, Byron, and Lord Tennyson, among others.

Spenser returned to Ireland and in 1591, Complaints, a collection of poems that voices complaints in mournful or mocking tones was published.

In 1595, Spenser published Amoretti and Epithalamion. The volume contains eighty-nine sonnets.

In the following year Spenser wrote a prose pamphlet titled A View of the Present State of Ireland, a highly inflammatory argument for the pacification and destruction of Irish culture.

On January 13th 1599 Edmund Spenser died at the age of forty-six. His coffin was carried to his grave in Westminster Abbey by other poets, who threw many pens and pieces of poetry into his grave followed with many tears.

Index of Contents
Book II. The Legend of Sir Guyon
Introductory Verses
Canto I
Canto II
Canto III
Canto IV
Canto V
Canto VI
Canto VII
Canto VIII
Canto IX
Canto X
Canto XI
Canto XII
Edmund Spenser – A Short Biography

Edmund Spenser – A Concise Bibliography

INTRODUCTORY VERSES

I
Right well I wote, most mighty Soveraine,
That all this famous antique history
Of some th' aboundance of an ydle braine
Will judged be, and painted forgery,
Rather then matter of just memory;
Sith none that breatheth living aire does know,
Where is that happy land of Faery,
Which I so much doe vaunt, yet no where show,
But vouch antiquities, which no body can know.

II
But let that man with better sence advize,
That of the world least part to us is red:
And daily how through hardy enterprize
Many great regions are discovered,
Which to late age were never mentioned.
Who ever heard of th' Indian Peru?
Or who in venturous vessell measured
The Amazons huge river, now found trew?
Or fruitfullest Virginia who did ever vew?

III
Yet all these were when no man did them know,
Yet have from wisest ages hidden beene;
And later times thinges more unknowne shall show.
Why then should witlesse man so much misweene,
That nothing is, but that which he hath seene?
What if within the moones fayre shining spheare,
What if in every other starre unseene,
Of other worldes he happily should heare?
He wonder would much more; yet such to some appeare.

IV
Of Faery Lond yet if he more inquyre,
By certein signes, here sett in sondrie place,
He may it fynd; ne let him then admyre,
But yield his sence to bee too blunt and bace,
That no'te without an hound fine footing trace.
And thou, O fayrest Princesse under sky,
In this fayre mirrhour maist behold thy face,
And thine owne realmes in lond of Faery,
And in this antique ymage thy great auncestry.

V

The which O pardon me thus to enfold
In covert vele, and wrap in shadowes light,
That feeble eyes your glory may behold,
Which ells could not endure those beames bright,
But would bee dazled with exceeding light.
O pardon! and vouchsafe with patient eare
The brave adventures of this Faery knight,
The good Sir Guyon, gratiously to heare;
In whom great rule of Temp'raunce goodly doth appeare.

CANTO I

Guyon, by Archimage abusd,
The Redcrosse Knight awaytes;
Fyndes Mordant and Amavia slaine
With Pleasures poisoned baytes.

I

That conning architect of cancred guyle,
Whom princes late displeasure left in bands,
For falsed letters and suborned wyle,
Soone as the Redcrosse Knight he understands
To beene departed out of Eden landes,
To serve againe his soveraine Elfin Queene,
His artes he moves, and out of caytives handes
Himselfe he frees by secret meanes unseene;
His shackles emptie lefte, him selfe escaped cleene.

II

And forth he fares full of malicious mynd,
To worken mischiefe and avenging woe,
Where ever he that godly knight may fynd,
His onely hart sore and his onely foe;
Sith Una now he algates must forgoe,
Whom his victorious handes did earst restore
To native crowne and kingdom late ygoe:
Where she enjoyes sure peace for evermore,
As wetherbeaten ship arryv'd on happie shore.

III

Him therefore now the object of his spight
And deadly food he makes: him to offend
By forged treason, or by open fight,
He seekes, of all his drifte the aymed end:
Thereto his subtile engins he does bend,
His practick witt, and his fayre fyled tonge,

With thousand other sleightes: for well he kend
His credit now in doubtfull ballaunce hong;
For hardly could bee hurt, who was already stong.

IV
Still as he went, he craftie stales did lay,
With cunning traynes him to entrap unwares,
And privy spyals plast in all his way,
To weete what course he takes, and how he fares;
To ketch him at a vauntage in his snares.
But now so wise and wary was the knight
By tryall of his former harmes and cares,
That he descryde, and shonned still his slight:
The fish that once was caught, new bait wil hardly byte.

V
Nath'lesse th' enchaunter would not spare his payne,
In hope to win occasion to his will;
Which when he long awaited had in vayne,
He chaungd his mynd from one to other ill:
For to all good he enimy was still.
Upon the way him fortuned to meet,
Fayre marching underneath a shady hill,
A goodly knight, all armd in harnesse meete,
That from his head no place appeared to his feete.

VI
His carriage was full comely and upright,
His countenance demure and temperate,
But yett so sterne and terrible in sight,
That cheard his friendes, and did his foes amate:
He was an Elfin borne, of noble state
And mickle worship in his native land;
Well could he tourney and in lists debate,
And knighthood tooke of good Sir Huons hand,
When with King Oberon he came to Fary Land.

VII
Him als accompanyd upon the way
A comely palmer, clad in black attyre,
Of rypest yeares, and heares all hoarie gray,
That with a staffe his feeble steps did stire,
Least his long way his aged limbes should tire:
And if by lookes one may the mind aread,
He seemd to be a sage and sober syre,
And ever with slow pace the knight did lead,
Who taught his trampling steed with equall steps to tread.

VIII
Such whenas Archimago them did view,
He weened well to worke some uncouth wyle,

Eftsoones, untwisting his deceiptfull clew,
He gan to weave a web of wicked guyle;
And with faire countenance and flattring style
To them approching, thus the knight bespake:
'Fayre sonne of Mars, that seeke with warlike spoyle,
And great atchiev'ments, great your selfe to make,
Vouchsafe to stay your steed for humble misers sake.'

IX
He stayd his steed for humble misers sake,
And badd tell on the tenor of his playnt;
Who feigning then in every limb to quake,
Through inward feare, and seeming pale and faynt,
With piteous mone his percing speach gan paynt:
'Deare lady, how shall I declare thy cace,
Whom late I left in languorous constraynt?
Would God, thy selfe now present were in place,
To tell this ruefull tale! Thy sight could win thee grace.

X
'Or rather would, O! would it so had chaunst,
That you, most noble sir, had present beene
When that lewd rybauld, with vyle lust advaunst,
Laid first his filthie hands on virgin cleene,
To spoyle her dainty corps, so faire and sheene
As on the earth, great mother of us all,
With living eye more fayre was never seene,
Of chastity and honour virginall:
Witnes, ye heavens, whom she in vaine to help did call.'

XI
'How may it be,' sayd then the knight halfe wroth,
'That knight should knighthood ever so have shent?'
'None but that saw,' quoth he, 'would weene for troth,
How shamefully that mayd he did torment.
Her looser golden lockes he rudely rent,
And drew her on the ground, and his sharpe sword
Against her snowy brest he fiercely bent,
And threatned death with many a bloodie word;
Tounge hates to tell the rest, that eye to see abhord.'

XII
Therewith amoved from his sober mood,
'And lives he yet,' said he, 'that wrought this act,
And doen the heavens afford him vitall food?'
'He lives,' quoth he, 'and boasteth of the fact,
Ne yet hath any knight his courage crackt.'
'Where may that treachour then,' sayd he, 'be found,
Or by what meanes may I his footing tract?'
'That shall I shew,' said he, 'as sure as hound
The stricken deare doth chaleng by the bleeding wound.'

XIII
He stayd not lenger talke, but with fierce yre
And zealous haste away is quickly gone,
To seeke that knight, where him that crafty squyre
Supposd to be. They do arrive anone,
Where sate a gentle lady all alone,
With garments rent, and heare discheveled,
Wringing her handes, and making piteous mone:
Her swollen eyes were much disfigured,
And her faire face with teares was fowly blubbered.

XIV
The knight, approching nigh, thus to her said:
'Fayre lady, through fowle sorrow ill bedight,
Great pitty is to see you thus dismayd,
And marre the blossom of your beauty bright:
Forthy appease your griefe and heavy plight,
And tell the cause of your conceived payne:
For if he live that hath you doen despight,
He shall you doe dew recompence agayne,
Or els his wrong with greater puissance maintaine.'

XV
Which when she heard, as in despightfull wise,
She wilfully her sorrow did augment,
And offred hope of comfort did despise:
Her golden lockes most cruelly she rent,
And scratcht her face with ghastly dreriment;
Ne would she speake, ne see, ne yet be seene,
But hid her visage, and her head downe bent,
Either for grievous shame, or for great teene,
As if her hart with sorow had transfixed beene:

XVI
Till her that squyre bespake: 'Madame, my liefe,
For Gods deare love be not so wilfull bent,
But doe vouchsafe now to receive reliefe,
The which good fortune doth to you present.
For what bootes it to weepe and to wayment,
When ill is chaunst, but doth the ill increase,
And the weake minde with double woe torment?'
When she her squyre heard speake, she gan appease
Her voluntarie paine, and feele some secret ease.

XVII
Eftsoone she said: 'Ah! gentle trustie squyre,
What comfort can I, wofull wretch, conceave,
Or why should ever I henceforth desyre
To see faire heavens face, and life not leave,
Sith that false traytour did my honour reave?'

'False traytour certes,' saide the Faerie knight,
'I read the man, that ever would deceave
A gentle lady, or her wrong through might:
Death were too little paine for such a fowle despight.

XVIII
'But now, fayre lady, comfort to you make,
And read who hath ye wrought this shamfull plight,
That short revenge the man may overtake,
Where so he be, and soone upon him light.'
'Certes,' saide she, 'I wote not how he hight,
But under him a gray steede did he wield,
Whose sides with dapled circles weren dight;
Upright he rode, and in his silver shield
He bore a bloodie crosse, that quartred all the field.'

XIX
'Now by my head,' saide Guyon, 'much I muse,
How that same knight should do so fowle amis,
Or ever gentle damzell so abuse:
For may I boldly say, he surely is
A right good knight, and trew of word ywis:
I present was, and can it witnesse well,
When armes he swore, and streight did enterpris
Th'adventure of the Errant Damozell;
In which he hath great glory wonne, as I heare tell.

XX
'Nathlesse he shortly shall againe be tryde,
And fairely quit him of th' imputed blame,
Els be ye sure he dearely shall abyde,
Or make you good amendment for the same:
All wrongs have mendes, but no amendes of shame.
Now therefore, lady, rise out of your paine,
And see the salving of your blotted name.'
Full loth she seemd thereto, but yet did faine;
For she was inly glad her purpose so to gaine.

XXI
Her purpose was not such as she did faine,
Ne yet her person such as it was seene;
But under simple shew and semblant plaine
Lurkt false Duessa secretly unseene,
As a chaste virgin, that had wronged beene:
So had false Archimago her disguysd,
To cloke her guile with sorrow and sad teene;
And eke himselfe had craftily devisd
To be her squire, and do her service well aguisd.

XXII
Her late, forlorne and naked, he had found,

Where she did wander in waste wildernesse,
Lurking in rockes and caves far under ground,
And with greene mosse cov'ring her nakednesse,
To hide her shame and loathly filthinesse,
Sith her Prince Arthur of proud ornaments
And borrowd beauty spoyld. Her nathelesse
Th'enchaunter finding fit for his intents
Did thus revest, and deckt with dew habiliments.

XXIII
For all he did was to deceive good knights,
And draw them from pursuit of praise and fame,
To slug in slouth and sensuall delights,
And end their daies with irrenowmed shame.
And now exceeding griefe him overcame,
To see the Redcrosse thus advaunced hye;
Therefore this craftie engine he did frame,
Against his praise to stirre up enmitye
Of such, as vertues like mote unto him allye.

XXIV
So now he Guyon guydes an uncouth way
Through woods and mountaines, till they came at last
Into a pleasant dale, that lowly lay
Betwixt two hils, whose high heads, overplast,
The valley did with coole shade overcast:
Through midst thereof a little river rold,
By which there sate a knight with helme unlaste,
Himselfe refreshing with the liquid cold,
After his travell long, and labours manifold.

XXV
'Lo! yonder he,' cryde Archimage alowd,
'That wrought the shamefull fact, which I did shew,
And now he doth himselfe in secret shrowd,
To fly the vengeaunce for his outrage dew;
But vaine: for ye shall dearely do him rew,
So God ye speed and send you good successe;
Which we far off will here abide to vew.'
So they him left, inflam'd with wrathfulnesse,
That streight against that knight his speare he did addresse.

XXVI
Who, seeing him from far so fierce to pricke,
His warlike armes about him gan embrace,
And in the rest his ready speare did sticke;
Tho, when as still he saw him towards pace,
He gan rencounter him in equall race:
They bene ymett, both ready to affrap,
When suddeinly that warriour gan abace
His threatned speare, as if some new mishap

Had him betide, or hidden danger did entrap:

XXVII
And cryde, 'Mercie, sir knight! and mercie, lord,
For mine offence and heedelesse hardiment,
That had almost committed crime abhord,
And with reprochfull shame mine honour shent,
Whiles cursed steele against that badge I bent,
The sacred badge of my Redeemers death,
Which on your shield is set for ornament.'
But his fierce foe his steed could stay uneath,
Who, prickt with courage kene, did cruell battell breath.

XXVIII
But when he heard him speake, streight way he knew
His errour, and himselfe inclyning sayd:
'Ah! deare Sir Guyon, well becommeth you,
But me behoveth rather to upbrayd,
Whose hastie hand so far from reason strayd,
That almost it did haynous violence
On that fayre ymage of that heavenly mayd,
That decks and armes your shield with faire defence:
Your court'sie takes on you anothers dew offence.'

XXIX
So beene they both at one, and doen upreare
Their bevers bright, each other for to greet;
Goodly comportaunce each to other beare,
And entertaine themselves with court'sies meet.
Then saide the Redcrosse Knight: 'Now mote I weet,
Sir Guyon, why with so fierce saliaunce,
And fell intent, ye did at earst me meet;
For sith I know your goodly governaunce,
Great cause, I weene, you guided, or some uncouth chaunce.'

XXX
'Certes,' said he, 'well mote I shame to tell
The fond encheason that me hether led.
A false infamous faitour late befell
Me for to meet, that seemed ill bested,
And playnd of grievous outrage, which he red
A knight had wrought against a ladie gent;
Which to avenge, he to this place me led,
Where you he made the marke of his intent,
And now is fled: foule shame him follow, wher he went!'

XXXI
So can he turne his earnest unto game,
Through goodly handling and wise temperaunce.
By this his aged guide in presence came,
Who, soone as on that knight his eye did glaunce,

Eftsoones of him had perfect cognizaunce,
Sith him in Faery court he late avizd;
And sayd: 'Fayre sonne, God give you happy chaunce,
And that deare Crosse uppon your shield devizd,
Wherewith above all knights ye goodly seeme aguizd.

XXXII
'Joy may you have, and everlasting fame,
Of late most hard atchiev'ment by you donne,
For which enrolled is your glorious name
In heavenly regesters above the sunne,
Where you a saint with saints your seat have wonne:
But wretched we, where ye have left your marke,
Must now anew begin like race to ronne.
God guide thee, Guyon, well to end thy warke,
And to the wished haven bring thy weary barke.'

XXXIII
'Palmer,' him answered the Redcrosse Knight,
'His be the praise, that this atchiev'ment wrought,
Who made my hand the organ of His might:
More then goodwill to me attribute nought;
For all I did, I did but as I ought.
But you, faire sir, whose pageant next ensewes,
Well mote yee thee, as well can wish your thought,
That home ye may report thrise happy newes;
For well ye worthy bene for worth and gentle thewes.'

XXXIV
So courteous conge both did give and take,
With right hands plighted, pledges of good will.
Then Guyon forward gan his voyage make
With his blacke palmer, that him guided still.
Still he him guided over dale and hill,
And with his steedy staffe did point his way:
His race with reason, and with words his will,
From fowle intemperaunce he ofte did stay,
And suffred not in wrath his hasty steps to stray.

XXXV
In this faire wize they traveild long yfere,
Through many hard assayes, which did betide,
Of which he honour still away did beare,
And spred his glory through all countryes wide.
At last, as chaunst them by a forest side
To passe, for succour from the scorching ray,
They heard a ruefull voice, that dearnly cride,
With percing shriekes, and many a dolefull lay;
Which to attend, a while their forward steps they stay.

XXXVI

'But if that carelesse hevens,' quoth she, 'despise
The doome of just revenge, and take delight
To see sad pageaunts of mens miseries,
As bownd by them to live in lives despight,
Yet can they not warne Death from wretched wight.
Come then, come soone, come, sweetest Death, to me,
And take away this long lent loathed light:
Sharpe be thy wounds, but sweete the medicines be,
That long captived soules from weary thraldome free.

XXXVII
'But thou, sweete babe, whom frowning froward fate
Hath made sad witnesse of thy fathers fall,
Sith heven thee deignes to hold in living state,
Long maist thou live, and better thrive withall,
Then to thy lucklesse parents did befall:
Live thou, and to thy mother dead attest,
That cleare she dide from blemish criminall:
Thy litle hands embrewd in bleeding brest,
Loe! I for pledges leave. So give me leave to rest.'

XXXVIII
With that a deadly shrieke she forth did throw,
That through the wood reechoed againe,
And after gave a grone so deepe and low,
That seemd her tender heart was rent in twaine,
Or thrild with point of thorough piercing paine:
As gentle hynd, whose sides with cruell steele
Through launched, forth her bleeding life does raine,
Whiles the sad pang approching shee does feele,
Braies out her latest breath, and up her eies doth seele.

XXXIX
Which when that warriour heard, dismounting straict
From his tall steed, he rusht into the thick,
And soone arrived where that sad pourtraict
Of death and dolour lay, halfe dead, halfe quick;
In whose white alabaster brest did stick
A cruell knife, that made a griesly wownd,
From which forth gusht a stream of goreblood thick,
That all her goodly garments staind arownd,
And into a deepe sanguine dide the grassy grownd.

XL
Pitifull spectacle of deadly smart,
Beside a bubling fountaine low she lay,
Which shee increased with her bleeding hart,
And the cleane waves with purple gore did ray;
Als in her lap a lovely babe did play
His cruell sport, in stead of sorrow dew;
For in her streaming blood he did embay

His litle hands, and tender joints embrew;
Pitifull spectacle, as ever eie did vew.

XLI
Besides them both, upon the soiled gras
Thedead corse of an armed knight was spred,
Whose armour all with blood besprincled was;
His ruddy lips did smyle, and rosy red
Did paint his chearefull cheekes, yett being ded;
Seemd to have beene a goodly personage,
Now in his freshest flowre of lustyhed,
Fitt to inflame faire lady with loves rage,
But that fiers fate did crop the blossome of his age.

XLII
Whom when the good Sir Guyon did behold,
His hart gan wexe as starke as marble stone,
And his fresh blood did frieze with fearefull cold,
That all his sences seemd berefte attone.
At last his mighty ghost gan deepe to grone,
As lion, grudging in his great disdaine,
Mournes inwardly, and makes to him selfe mone,
Til ruth and fraile affection did constraine
His stout courage to stoupe, and shew his inward paine.

XLIII
Out of her gored wound the cruell steel
He lightly snatcht, and did the floodgate stop
With his faire garment: then gan softly feel
Her feeble pulse, to prove if any drop
Of living blood yet in her veynes did hop;
Which when he felt to move, he hoped faire
To call backe life to her forsaken shop:
So well he did her deadly wounds repaire,
That at the last shee gan to breath out living aire.

XLIV
Which he perceiving, greatly gan rejoice,
And goodly counsell, that for wounded hart
Is meetest med'cine, tempred with sweete voice:
'Ay me! deare lady, which the ymage art
Of ruefull pitty, and impatient smart,
What direfull chaunce, armd with avenging fate,
Or cursed hand, hath plaid this cruell part,
Thus fowle to hasten your untimely date?
Speake, O dear lady, speake: help never comes too late.'

XLV
Therewith her dim eie-lids she up gan reare,
On which the drery death did sitt, as sad
As lump of lead, and made darke clouds appeare:

But when as him, all in bright armour clad,
Before her standing she espied had,
As one out of a deadly dreame affright,
She weakely started, yet she nothing drad:
Streight downe againe her selfe in great despight
She groveling threw to ground, as hating life and light.

XLVI
The gentle knight her soone with carefull paine
Uplifted light, and softly did uphold:
Thrise he her reard, and thrise she sunck againe,
Till he his armes about her sides gan fold,
And to her said: 'Yet if the stony cold
Have not all seized on your frozen hart,
Let one word fall that may your griefe unfold,
And tell the secrete of your mortall smart:
He oft finds present helpe, who does his griefe impart.'

XLVII
Then, casting up a deadly looke, full low
Shee sight from bottome of her wounded brest,
And after, many bitter throbs did throw:
With lips full pale and foltring tong opprest,
These words she breathed forth from riven chest:
'Leave, ah! leave of, what ever wight thou bee,
To lett a weary wretch from her dew rest,
And trouble dying soules tranquilitee.
Take not away now got, which none would give to me.'

XLVIII
'Ah! far be it,' said he, 'deare dame, fro mee,
To hinder soule from her desired rest,
Or hold sad life in long captivitee:
For all I seeke is but to have redrest
The bitter pangs that doth your heart infest.
Tell then, O lady, tell what fatall priefe
Hath with so huge misfortune you opprest:
That I may cast to compas your reliefe,
Or die with you in sorrow, and partake your griefe.'

XLIX
With feeble hands then stretched forth on hye,
As heven accusing guilty of her death,
And with dry drops congealed in her eye,
In these sad wordes she spent her utmost breath:
'Heare then, O man, the sorrowes that uneath
My tong can tell, so far all sence they pas:
Loe! this dead corpse, that lies here underneath,
The gentlest knight, that ever on greene gras
Gay steed with spurs did pricke, the good Sir Mortdant was.

links to the figure of Morganna Le Fay

L
'Was (ay the while, that he is not so now!)
My lord, my love, my deare lord, my deare love,
So long as hevens just with equall brow
Vouchsafed to behold us from above.
One day, when him high corage did emmove,
As wont ye knightes to seeke adventures wilde,
He pricked forth, his puissant force to prove.
Me then he left enwombed of this childe,
This luckles childe, whom thus ye see with blood defild.

LI
'Him fortuned (hard fortune ye may ghesse)
To come where vile Acrasia does wonne,
Acrasia, a false enchaunteresse,
That many errant knightes hath fowle fordonne:
Within a wandring island, that doth ronne
And stray in perilous gulfe, her dwelling is:
Fayre sir, if ever there ye travell, shonne
The cursed land where many wend amis,
And know it by the name; it hight the Bowre of Blis.

the sexual and seductive woman

LII
'**Her blis is all in pleasure and delight,**
Wherewith she makes her lovers dronken mad,
And then with words and weedes of wondrous might,
On them she workes her will to uses bad:
My liefest lord **she thus beguiled had;**
For he was flesh (all flesh doth frayltie breed):
Whom when I heard to beene so ill bestad,
Weake wretch, I wrapt myselfe in palmers weed,
And cast to seek him forth through danger and great dreed.

LIII
'Now had fayre Cynthia by even tournes
Full measured three quarters of her yeare,
And thrise three tymes had fild her crooked hornes,
Whenas my wombe her burdein would forbeare,
And bad me call Lucina to me neare.
Lucina came: a manchild forth I brought:
The woods, the nymphes, my bowres, my midwives, weare:
Hard helpe at need! So deare thee, babe, I bought;
Yet nought to dear I deemd, while so my deare I sought.

doesn't conform so is a witch

LIV
'Him so I sought, and so at last I fownd,
Where him that witch had thralled to her will,
In chaines of lust and lewde desyres ybownd,
And so transformed from his former skill,
That me he knew not, nether his owne ill;
Till through wise handling and faire governaunce,

I him recured to a better will,
Purged from drugs of fowle intemperaunce:
Then meanes I gan devise for his deliveraunce.

LV

'Which when the vile enchaunteresse perceiv'd,
How that my lord from her I would reprive,
With cup thus charmd, him parting she deceivd:
Sad verse, give death to him that death does give,
And losse of love to her that loves to live,
So soone as Bacchus with the Nymphe does lincke.
So parted we, and on our journey drive,
Till, comming to this well, he stoupt to drincke:
The charme fulfild, dead suddeinly he downe did sincke.

[margin note: says she murdered the man out of jealousy]

LVI

'Which when I, wretch'—Not one word more she sayd,
But breaking of the end for want of breath,
And slyding soft, as downe to sleepe her layd,
And ended all her woe in quiet death.
That seeing good Sir Guyon, could uneath
From teares abstayne, for griefe his hart did grate,
And from so heavie sight his head did wreath,
Accusing fortune, and too cruell fate,
Which plonged had faire lady in so wretched state.

LVII

Then, turning to his palmer, said: 'Old syre,
Behold the ymage of mortalitie,
And feeble nature cloth'd with fleshly tyre.
When raging passion with fierce tyranny
Robs reason of her dew regalitie,
And makes it servaunt to her basest part,
The strong it weakens with infirmitie,
And with bold furie armes the weakest hart:
The strong through pleasure soonest falles, the weake through smart.'

LVIII

'But Temperaunce,' said he, 'with golden squire
Betwixt them both can measure out a meane,
Nether to melt in pleasures whott desyre,
Nor frye in hartlesse griefe and dolefull tene.
Thrise happy man, who fares them both atweene!
But sith this wretched woman overcome
Of anguish, rather then of crime, hath bene,
Reserve her cause to her eternall doome,
And, in the meane, vouchsafe her honorable toombe.'

LIX

'Palmer,' quoth he, 'death is an equall doome
To good and bad, the commen in of rest;

But after death the tryall is to come,
When best shall bee to them that lived best:
But both alike, when death hath both suppresst,
Religious reverence doth buriall teene,
Which who so wants, wants so much of his rest:
For all so great shame after death I weene,
As selfe to dyen bad, unburied bad to beene.'

LX
So both agree their bodies to engrave:
The great earthes wombe they open to the sky,
And with sad cypresse seemely it embrave;
Then, covering with a clod their closed eye,
They lay therein those corses tenderly,
And bid them sleepe in everlasting peace.
But ere they did their utmost obsequy,
Sir Guyon, more affection to increace,
Bynempt a sacred vow, which none should ay releace.

LXI
The dead knights sword out of his sheath he drew,
With which he cutt a lock of all their heare,
Which medling with their blood and earth, he threw
Into the grave, and gan devoutly sweare:
'Such and such evil God on Guyon reare,
And worse and worse, young orphane, be thy payne,
If I or thou dew vengeance doe forbeare,
Till guiltie blood her guerdon doe obtayne.'
So shedding many teares, they closd the earth agayne.

swears vengeance against Acrasia

CANTO II

Babes bloody handes may not be clensd:
The face of Golden Meane:
Her sisters, two Extremities,
Strive her to banish cleane.

I
Thus when Sir Guyon, with his faithful guyde,
Had with dew rites and dolorous lament
The end of their sad tragedie uptyde,
The litle babe up in his armes he hent;
Who, with sweet pleasaunce and bold blandishment,
Gan smyle on them, that rather ought to weepe,
As carelesse of his woe, or innocent
Of that was doen; that ruth emperced deepe
In that knightes hart, and wordes with bitter teares did steepe:

II

'Ah! lucklesse babe, borne under cruell starre,
And in dead parents balefull ashes bred,
Full little weenest thou, what sorrowes are
Left thee for porcion of thy livelyhed:
Poore orphane! in the wide world scattered,
As budding braunch rent from the native tree,
And throwen forth, till it be withered!
Such is the state of men! Thus enter we
Into this life with woe, and end with miseree!'

III

Then soft him selfe inclyning on his knee
Downe to that well, did in the water weene
(So love does loath disdainefull nicitee)
His guiltie handes from bloody gore to cleene.
He washt them oft and oft, yet nought they beene
For all his washing cleaner. Still he strove,
Yet still the litle hands were bloody seene:
The which him into great amaz'ment drove,
And into diverse doubt his wavering wonder clove.

IV

He wist not whether blott of fowle offence
Might not be purgd with water nor with bath;
Or that High God, in lieu of innocence,
Imprinted had that token of his wrath,
To shew how sore bloodguiltinesse he hat'th;
Or that the charme and veneme, which they dronck,
Their blood with secret filth infected hath,
Being diffused through the sencelesse tronck,
That, through the great contagion, direful deadly stonck.

V

Whom thus at gaze the palmer gan to bord
With goodly reason, and thus fayre bespake:
'Ye bene right hard amated, gratious lord,
And of your ignorance great merveill make,
Whiles cause not well conceived ye mistake.
But know, that secret vertues are infusd
In every fountaine, and in everie lake,
Which who hath skill them rightly to have chusd
To proofe of passing wonders hath full often usd.

VI

'Of those some were so from their sourse indewd
By great Dame Nature, from whose fruitfull pap
Their welheads spring, and are with moisture deawd;
Which feedes each living plant with liquid sap,
And filles with flowres fayre Floraes painted lap:

But other some by guifte of later grace,
Or by good prayers, or by other hap,
Had vertue pourd into their waters bace,
And thenceforth were renowmd, and sought from place to place.

VII
'Such is this well, wrought by occasion straunge,
Which to her nymph befell. Upon a day,
As she the woodes with bow and shaftes did raunge,
The hartlesse hynd and robucke to dismay,
Dan Faunus chaunst to meet her by the way,
And kindling fire at her faire burning eye,
Inflamed was to follow beauties pray,
And chaced her, that fast from him did fly;
As hynd from her, so she fled from her enimy.

VIII
'At last, when fayling breath began to faint,
And saw no meanes to scape, of shame affrayd,
She set her downe to weepe for sore constraint,
And to Diana calling lowd for ayde,
Her deare besought, to let her die a mayd.
The goddesse heard, and suddeine, where she sate,
Welling out streames of teares, and quite dismayd
With stony feare of that rude rustick mate,
Transformd her to a stone from stedfast virgins state.

IX
'Lo! now she is that stone, from whose two heads,
As from two weeping eyes, fresh streames do flow,
Yet colde through feare and old conceived dreads;
And yet the stone her semblance seemes to show,
Shapt like a maide, that such ye may her know;
And yet her vertues in her water byde;
For it is chaste and pure, as purest snow,
Ne lets her waves with any filth be dyde,
But ever like her selfe unstayned hath beene tryde.

X
'From thence it comes, that this babes bloody hand
May not be clensd with water of this well:
Ne certes, sir, strive you it to withstand,
But let them still be bloody, as befell,
That they his mothers innocence may tell,
As she bequeathd in her last testament;
That as a sacred symbole it may dwell
In her sonnes flesh, to mind revengement,
And be for all chaste dames an endlesse moniment.'

XI
He harkned to his reason, and the childe

Uptaking, to the palmer gave to beare;
But his sad fathers armes with blood defilde,
An heavie load, himselfe did lightly reare;
And turning to that place, in which whyleare
He left his loftie steed with golden sell
And goodly gorgeous barbes, him found not theare:
By other accident, that earst befell,
He is convaide; but how or where, here fits not tell.

XII
Which when Sir Guyon saw, all were he wroth,
Yet algates mote he soft himselfe appease,
And fairely fare on foot, how ever loth:
His double burden did him sore disease.
So long they traveiled with litle ease,
Till that at last they to a castle came,
Built on a rocke adjoyning to the seas:
It was an auncient worke of antique fame,
And wondrous strong by nature, and by skilfull frame.

XIII
Therein three sisters dwelt of sundry sort,
The children of one syre by mothers three;
Who dying whylome did divide this fort
To them by equall shares in equall fee:
But stryfull mind and diverse qualitee
Drew them in partes, and each made others foe:
Still did they strive, and daily disagree;
The eldest did against the youngest goe,
And both against the middest meant to worken woe.

XIV
Where when the knight arriv'd, he was right well
Receiv'd, as knight of so much worth became,
Of second sister, who did far excell
The other two; Medina was her name,
A sober sad, and comely courteous dame;
Who, rich arayd, and yet in modest guize,
In goodly garments, that her well became,
Fayre marching forth in honorable wize,
Him at the threshold mett, and well did enterprize.

XV
She led him up into a goodly bowre,
And comely courted with meet modestie,
Ne in her speach, ne in her haviour,
Was lightnesse seene, or looser vanitie,
But gratious womanhood, and gravitie,
Above the reason of her youthly yeares:
Her golden lockes she roundly did uptye
In breaded tramels, that no looser heares

Did out of order stray about her daintie eares.

XVI
Whilest she her selfe thus busily did frame,
Seemely to entertaine her new-come guest,
Newes hereof to her other sisters came,
Who all this while were at their wanton rest,
Accourting each her frend with lavish fest:
They were two knights of perelesse puissaunce,
And famous far abroad for warlike gest,
Which to these ladies love did countenaunce,
And to his mistresse each himselfe strove to advaunce.

XVII
He that made love unto the eldest dame
Was hight Sir Huddibras, an hardy man;
Yet not so good of deedes as great of name,
Which he by many rash adventures wan,
Since errant armes to sew he first began:
More huge in strength then wise in workes he was,
And reason with foole-hardize over ran;
Sterne melancholy did his courage pas;
And was, for terrour more, all armd in shyning bras.

XVIII
But he that lov'd the youngest was Sansloy,
He that faire Una late fowle outraged,
The most unruly and the boldest boy,
That ever warlike weapons menaged,
And to all lawlesse lust encouraged
Through strong opinion of his matchlesse might;
Ne ought he car'd, whom he endamaged
By tortious wrong, or whom bereav'd of right.
He now this ladies champion chose for love to fight.

XIX
These two gay knights, vowd to so diverse loves,
Each other does envy with deadly hate,
And daily warre against his foeman moves,
In hope to win more favour with his mate,
And th' others pleasing service to abate,
To magnifie his owne. But when they heard,
How in that place straunge knight arrived late,
Both knights and ladies forth right angry far'd,
And fercely unto battell sterne themselves prepar'd.

XX
But ere they could proceede unto the place
Where he abode, themselves at discord fell,
And cruell combat joynd in middle space:
With horrible assault, and fury fell,

They heapt huge strokes, the scorned life to quell,
That all on uprore from her settled seat
The house was raysd, and all that in did dwell;
Seemd that lowde thunder with amazement great
Did rend the ratling skyes with flames of fouldering heat.

XXI

The noyse thereof cald forth that straunger knight,
To weet what dreadfull thing was there in hand;
Where when as two brave knightes in bloody fight
With deadly rancour he enraunged fond,
His sunbroad shield about his wrest he bond,
And shyning blade unsheathd, with which he ran
Unto that stead, their strife to understond;
And at his first arrivall, them began
With goodly meanes to pacifie, well as he can.

XXII

But they him spying, both with greedy forse
Attonce upon him ran, and him beset
With strokes of mortall steele without remorse,
And on his shield like yron sledges bet:
As when a beare and tygre, being met
In cruell fight on Lybicke ocean wide,
Espye a traveiler with feet surbet,
Whom they in equall pray hope to divide,
They stint their strife, and him assayle on everie side.

XXIII

But he, not like a weary traveilere,
Their sharp assault right boldly did rebut,
And suffred not their blowes to byte him nere,
But with redoubled buffes them backe did put:
Whose grieved mindes, which choler did englut,
Against themselves turning their wrathfull spight,
Gan with new rage their shieldes to hew and cut;
But still when Guyon came to part their fight,
With heavie load on him they freshly gan to smight.

XXIV

As a tall ship tossed in troublous seas,
Whom raging windes, threatning to make the pray
Of the rough rockes, doe diversly disease,
Meetes two contrarie billowes by the way,
That her on either side doe sore assay,
And boast to swallow her in greedy grave;
Shee, scorning both their spights, does make wide way,
And with her brest breaking the fomy wave,
Does ride on both their backs, and faire her self doth save:

XXV

So boldly he him beares, and rusheth forth
Betweene them both, by conduct of his blade.
Wondrous great prowesse and heroick worth
He shewd that day, and rare ensample made,
When two so mighty warriours he dismade:
Attonce he wards and strikes, he takes and paies,
Now forst to yield, now forcing to invade,
Before, behind, and round about him laies:
So double was his paines, so double be his praise.

XXVI
Straunge sort of fight, three valiaunt knights to see
Three combates joine in one, and to darraine
A triple warre with triple enmitee,
All for their ladies froward love to gaine,
Which gotten was but hate. So Love does raine
In stoutest minds, and maketh monstrous warre;
He maketh warre, he maketh peace againe,
And yett his peace is but continuall jarre:
O miserable men, that to him subject arre!

XXVII
Whilst thus they mingled were in furious armes,
The faire Medina, with her tresses torne
And naked brest, in pitty of their harmes,
Emongst them ran, and, falling them beforne,
Besought them by the womb, which them had born,
And by the loves, which were to them most deare,
And by the knighthood, which they sure had sworn,
Their deadly cruell discord to forbeare,
And to her just conditions of faire peace to heare.

XXVIII
But her two other sisters, standing by,
Her lowd gainsaid, and both their champions bad
Pursew the end of their strong enmity,
As ever of their loves they would be glad.
Yet she with pitthy words and counsell sad
Still strove their stubborne rages to revoke,
That, at the last, suppressing fury mad,
They gan abstaine from dint of direfull stroke,
And hearken to the sober speaches which she spoke.

XXIX
'Ah! puissaunt lords, what cursed evill spright,
Or fell Erinnys, in your noble harts
Her hellish brond hath kindled with despight,
And stird you up to worke your wilfull smarts?
Is this the joy of armes? be these the parts
Of glorious knighthood, after blood to thrust,
And not regard dew right and just desarts?

Vaine is the vaunt, and victory unjust,
That more to mighty hands then rightfull cause doth trust.

XXX
'And were there rightfull cause of difference,
Yet were not better, fayre it to accord,
Then with bloodguiltinesse to heape offence,
And mortal vengeaunce joyne to crime abhord?
O fly from wrath! fly, O my liefest lord!
Sad be the sights, and bitter fruites of warre,
And thousand furies wait on wrathfull sword;
Ne ought the praise of prowesse more doth marre
Then fowle revenging rage, and base contentious jarre.

XXXI
'But lovely concord, and most sacred peace,
Doth nourish vertue, and fast friendship breeds;
Weake she makes strong, and strong thing does increace,
Till it the pitch of highest praise exceeds;
Brave be her warres, and honorable deeds,
By which she triumphes over yre and pride,
And winnes an olive girlond for her meeds:
Be therefore, O my deare lords, pacifide,
And this misseeming discord meekely lay aside.'

XXXII
Her gracious words their rancour did appall,
And suncke so deepe into their boyling brests,
That downe they lett their cruell weapons fall,
And lowly did abase their lofty crests
To her faire presence and discrete behests.
Then she began a treaty to procure,
And stablish termes betwixt both their requests,
That as a law for ever should endure;
Which to observe, in word of knights they did assure.

XXXIII
Which to confirme, and fast to bind their league,
After their weary sweat and bloody toile,
She them besought, during their quiet treague,
Into her lodging to repaire a while,
To rest themselves, and grace to reconcile.
They soone consent: so forth with her they fare,
Where they are well receivd, and made to spoile
Themselves of soiled armes, and to prepare
Their minds to pleasure, and their mouths to dainty fare.

XXXIV
And those two froward sisters, their faire loves,
Came with them eke, all were they wondrous loth,
And fained cheare, as for the time behoves;

But could not colour yet so well the troth,
But that their natures bad appeard in both:
For both did at their second sister grutch,
And inly grieve, as doth an hidden moth
The inner garment frett, not th' utter touch;
One thought her cheare too litle, th' other thought too mutch.

XXXV
Elissa (so the eldest hight) did deeme
Such entertainment base, ne ought would eat,
Ne ought would speake, but evermore did seeme
As discontent for want of merth or meat;
No solace could her paramour intreat
Her once to show, ne court, nor dalliaunce;
But with bent lowring browes, as she would threat,
She scould, and frownd with froward countenaunce,
Unworthy of faire ladies comely governaunce.

XXXVI
But young Perissa was of other mynd,
Full of disport, still laughing, loosely light,
And quite contrary to her sisters kynd;
No measure in her mood, no rule of right,
But poured out in pleasure and delight;
In wine and meats she flowd above the banck,
And in excesse exceeded her owne might;
In sumptuous tire she joyd her selfe to pranck,
But of her love too lavish (litle have she thanck.)

XXXVII
Fast by her side did sitt the bold Sansloy,
Fitt mate for such a mincing mineon,
Who in her loosenesse tooke exceeding joy;
Might not be found a francker franion,
Of her leawd parts to make companion:
But Huddibras, more like a malecontent,
Did see and grieve at his bold fashion;
Hardly could he endure his hardiment,
Yett still he satt, and inly did him selfe torment.

XXXVIII
Betwixt them both the faire Medina sate
With sober grace and goodly carriage:
With equall measure she did moderate
The strong extremities of their outrage.
That forward paire she ever would asswage,
When they would strive dew reason to exceed;
But that same froward twaine would accorage,
And of her plenty adde unto their need:
So kept she them in order, and her selfe in heed.

XXXIX
Thus fairely shee attempered her feast,
And pleasd them all with meete satiety:
At last, when lust of meat and drinke was ceast,
She Guyon deare besought of curtesie,
To tell from whence he came through jeopardy,
And whether now on new adventure bownd:
Who with bold grace, and comely gravity,
Drawing to him the eies of all arownd,
From lofty siege began these words aloud to sownd.

XL
'This thy demaund, O lady, doth revive
Fresh memory in me of that great Queene,
Great and most glorious virgin Queene alive,
That with her soveraine powre, and scepter shene,
All Faery Lond does peaceably sustene.
In widest ocean she her throne does reare,
That over all the earth it may be seene;
As morning sunne her beames dispredden cleare,
And in her face faire peace and mercy doth appeare.

XLI
'In her the richesse of all heavenly grace
In chiefe degree are heaped up on hye:
And all, that els this worlds enclosure bace
Hath great or glorious in mortall eye,
Adornes the person of her Majestye;
That men beholding so great excellence,
And rare perfection in mortalitye,
Doe her adore with sacred reverence,
As th' idole of her Makers great magnificence.

XLII
'To her I homage and my service owe,
In number of the noblest knightes on ground,
Mongst whom on me she deigned to bestowe
Order of Maydenhead, the most renownd,
That may this day in all the world be found.
An yearely solemne feast she wontes to hold,
The day that first doth lead the yeare around;
To which all knights of worth and courage bold
Resort, to heare of straunge adventures to be told.

XLIII
'There this old palmer shewd himselfe that day,
And to that mighty Princesse did complaine
Of grievous mischiefes, which a wicked Fay
Had wrought, and many whelmd in deadly paine,
Whereof he crav'd redresse. My soveraine,
Whose glory is in gracious deeds, and joyes

Throughout the world her mercy to maintaine,
Eftsoones devisd redresse for such annoyes:
Me, all unfitt for so great purpose, she employes.

XLIV
'Now hath faire Phebe with her silver face
Thrise seene the shadowes of the neather world,
Sith last I left that honorable place,
In which her roiall presence is enrold;
Ne ever shall I rest in house nor hold,
Till I that false Acrasia have wonne;
Of whose fowle deedes, too hideous to bee told,
I witnesse am, and this their wretched sonne,
Whose wofull parents she hath wickedly fordonne.'

XLV
'Tell on, fayre sir,' said she, 'that dolefull tale,
From which sad ruth does seeme you to restraine,
That we may pitty such unhappie bale,
And learne from Pleasures poyson to abstaine:
Ill by ensample good doth often gayne.'
Then forward he his purpose gan pursew,
And told the story of the mortall payne,
Which Mordant and Amavia did rew;
As with lamenting eyes him selfe did lately vew.

XLVI
Night was far spent, and now in ocean deep
Orion, flying fast from hissing Snake,
His flaming head did hasten for to steep,
When of his pitteous tale he end did make;
Whilst with delight of that he wisely spake
Those guestes beguyled did beguyle their eyes
Of kindly sleepe, that did them overtake.
At last, when they had markt the chaunged skyes,
They wist their houre was spent; then each to rest him hyes.

CANTO III

Vaine Braggadocchio, getting Guyons
horse, is made the scorne
Of knighthood trew, and is of fayre
Belphœbe fowle forlorne.

I
Soone as the morrow fayre with purple beames
Disperst the shadowes of the misty night,

And Titan, playing on the eastern streames,
Gan cleare the deawy ayre with springing light,
Sir Guyon, mindfull of his vow yplight,
Uprose from drowsie couch, and him addrest
Unto the journey which he had behight:
His puissaunt armes about his noble brest,
And many-folded shield he bound about his wrest.

II
Then taking congè of that virgin pure,
The bloody-handed babe unto her truth
Did earnestly committ, and her conjure,
In vertuous lore to traine his tender youth,
And all that gentle noriture ensueth:
And that, so soone as ryper yeares he raught,
He might, for memory of that dayes ruth,
Be called Ruddymane, and thereby taught
T' avenge his parents death on them that had it wrought.

III
So forth he far'd, as now befell, on foot,
Sith his good steed is lately from him gone;
Patience perforce: helplesse what may it boot
To frett for anger, or for griefe to mone?
His palmer now shall foot no more alone.
So fortune wrought, as under greene woodes syde
He lately hard that dying lady grone,
He left his steed without, and speare besyde,
And rushed in on foot to ayd her, ere she dyde.

IV
The whyles a losell wandring by the way,
One that to bountie never cast his mynd,
Ne thought of honour ever did assay
His baser brest, but in his kestrell kynd
A pleasing vaine of glory he did fynd,
To which his flowing toung and troublous spright
Gave him great ayd, and made him more inclynd:
He, that brave steed there finding ready dight,
Purloynd both steed and speare, and ran away full light.

V
Now gan his hart all swell in jollity,
And of him selfe great hope and help conceiv'd,
That puffed up with smoke of vanity,
And with selfe-loved personage deceiv'd,
He gan to hope of men to be receiv'd
For such as he him thought, or faine would bee:
But for in court gay portaunce he perceiv'd
And gallant shew to be in greatest gree,
Eftsoones to court he cast t' advaunce his first degree.

VI
And by the way he chaunced to espy
One sitting ydle on a sunny banck,
To whom avaunting in great bravery,
As peacocke, that his painted plumes doth pranck,
He smote his courser in the trembling flanck,
And to him threatned his hart-thrilling speare:
The seely man, seeing him ryde so ranck
And ayme at him, fell flatt to ground for feare,
And crying 'Mercy!' loud, his pitious handes gan reare.

VII
Thereat the scarcrow wexed wondrous prowd,
Through fortune of his first adventure fayre,
And with big thundring voice revyld him lowd:
'Vile caytive, vassall of dread and despayre,
Unworthie of the commune breathed ayre,
Why livest thou, dead dog, a lenger day,
And doest not unto death thy selfe prepayre?
Dy, or thy selfe my captive yield for ay;
Great favour I thee graunt, for aunswere thus to stay.'

VIII
'Hold, O deare lord, hold your dead-doing hand!'
Then loud he cryde, 'I am your humble thrall.'
'Ah, wretch!' quoth he, 'thy destinies withstand
My wrathfull will, and doe for mercy call.
I give thee life: therefore prostrated fall,
And kisse my stirrup; that thy homage bee.'
The miser threw him selfe, as an offall,
Streight at his foot in base humilitee,
And cleeped him his liege, to hold of him in fee.

IX
So happy peace they made and faire accord.
Eftsoones this liegeman gan to wexe more bold,
And when he felt the folly of his lord,
In his owne kind he gan him selfe unfold:
For he was wylie witted, and growne old
In cunning sleightes and practick knavery.
From that day forth he cast for to uphold
His ydle humour with fine flattery,
And blow the bellowes to his swelling vanity.

X
Trompart, fitt man for Braggadochio,
To serve at court in view of vaunting eye;
Vaineglorious man, when fluttring wind does blow
In his light winges, is lifted up to skye;
The scorne of knighthood and trew chevalrye,

To thinke, without desert of gentle deed
And noble worth, to be advaunced hye:
Such prayse is shame; but honour, vertues meed,
Doth beare the fayrest flowre in honourable seed.

XI
So forth they pas, a well consorted payre,
Till that at length with Archimage they meet:
Who, seeing one that shone in armour fayre,
On goodly courser thondring with his feet,
Eftsoones supposed him a person meet
Of his revenge to make the instrument:
For since the Redcrosse Knight he erst did weet,
To beene with Guyon knitt in one consent,
The ill, which earst to him, he now to Guyon ment.

XII
And comming close to Trompart gan inquere
Of him, what mightie warriour that mote bee,
That rode in golden sell with single spere,
But wanted sword to wreake his enmitee.
'He is a great adventurer,' said he,
'That hath his sword through hard assay forgone,
And now hath vowd, till he avenged bee
Of that despight, never to wearen none;
That speare is him enough to doen a thousand grone.'

XIII
Th' enchaunter greatly joyed in the vaunt,
And weened well ere long his will to win,
And both his foen with equall foyle to daunt.
Tho to him louting lowly did begin
To plaine of wronges, which had committed bin
By Guyon, and by that false Redcrosse Knight,
Which two, through treason and deceiptfull gin,
Had slayne Sir Mordant and his lady bright:
That mote him honour win, to wreak so foule despight.

XIV
Therewith all suddeinly he seemd enragd,
And threatned death with dreadfull countenaunce,
As if their lives had in his hand beene gagd;
And with stiffe force shaking his mortall launce,
To let him weet his doughtie valiaunce,
Thus said: 'Old man, great sure shalbe thy meed,
If, where those knights for feare of dew vengeaunce
Doe lurke, thou certeinly to mee areed,
That I may wreake on them their hainous hateful deed.'

XV
'Certes, my lord,' said he, 'that shall I soone,

And give you eke good helpe to their decay.
But mote I wisely you advise to doon,
Give no ods to your foes, but doe purvay
Your selfe of sword before that bloody day:
For they be two the prowest knights on grownd,
And oft approv'd in many hard assay;
And eke of surest steele, that may be fownd,
Doe arme your self against that day, them to confownd.'

XVI
'Dotard,' saide he, 'let be thy deepe advise;
Seemes that through many yeares thy wits thee faile,
And that weake eld hath left thee nothing wise,
Els never should thy judgement be so frayle,
To measure manhood by the sword or mayle.
Is not enough fowre quarters of a man,
Withouten sword or shield, an hoste to quayle?
Thou litle wotest what this right-hand can:
Speake they, which have beheld the battailes which it wan.'

XVII
The man was much abashed at his boast;
Yet well he wist, that who so would contend
With either of those knightes on even coast,
Should neede of all his armes, him to defend;
Yet feared least his boldnesse should offend:
When Braggadocchio saide: 'Once I did sweare,
When with one sword seven knightes I brought to end,
Thence forth in battaile never sword to beare,
But it were that which noblest knight on earth doth weare.'

XVIII
'Perdy, sir knight,' saide then th' enchaunter blive,
'That shall I shortly purchase to your hond:
For now the best and noblest knight alive
Prince Arthur is, that wonnes in Faerie Lond;
He hath a sword, that flames like burning brond.
The same, by my device, I undertake
Shall by to morrow by thy side be fond.'
At which bold word that boaster gan to quake,
And wondred in his minde what mote that monster make.

XIX
He stayd not for more bidding, but away
Was suddein vanished out of his sight:
The northerne winde his wings did broad display
At his commaund, and reared him up light
From of the earth to take his aerie flight.
They lookt about, but no where could espye
Tract of his foot: then dead through great affright
They both nigh were, and each bad other flye:

Both fled attonce, ne ever backe retourned eye:

XX
Till that they come unto a forrest greene,
In which they shrowd themselves from causeles feare;
Yet feare them followes still, where so they beene.
Each trembling leafe and whistling wind they heare,
As ghastly bug, their haire on end does reare:
Yet both doe strive their fearefulnesse to faine.
At last they heard a horne, that shrilled cleare
Throughout the wood, that ecchoed againe,
And made the forrest ring, as it would rive in twaine.

XXI
Eft through the thicke they heard one rudely rush;
With noyse whereof he from his loftie steed
Downe fell to ground, and crept into a bush,
To hide his coward head from dying dreed.
But Trompart stoutly stayd to taken heed
Of what might hap. Eftsoone there stepped foorth
A goodly ladie clad in hunters weed,
That seemd to be a woman of great worth,
And, by her stately portance, borne of heavenly birth.

XXII
Her face so faire as flesh it seemed not,
But hevenly pourtraict of bright angels hew,
Cleare as the skye, withouten blame or blot,
Through goodly mixture of complexions dew;
And in her cheekes the vermeill red did shew
Like roses in a bed of lillies shed,
The which ambrosiall odours from them threw,
And gazers sense with double pleasure fed,
Hable to heale the sicke, and to revive the ded.

XXIII
In her faire eyes two living lamps did flame,
Kindled above at th' Hevenly Makers light,
And darted fyrie beames out of the same,
So passing persant, and so wondrous bright,
That quite bereav'd the rash beholders sight:
In them the blinded god his lustfull fyre
To kindle oft assayd, but had no might;
For with dredd majestie and awfull yre
She broke his wanton darts, and quenched bace desyre.

XXIV
Her yvorie forhead, full of bountie brave,
Like a broad table did it selfe dispred,
For Love his loftie triumphes to engrave,
And write the battailes of his great godhed:

All good and honour might therein be red:
For there their dwelling was. And when she spake,
Sweete wordes, like dropping honny, she did shed,
And twixt the perles and rubins softly brake
A silver sound, that heavenly musicke seemd to make.

XXV
Upon her eyelids many Graces sate,
Under the shadow of her even browes,
Working belgardes and amorous retrate,
And everie one her with a grace endowes,
And everie one with meekenesse to her bowes.
So glorious mirrhour of celestiall grace,
And soveraine moniment of mortall vowes,
How shall frayle pen descrive her heavenly face,
For feare, through want of skill, her beauty to disgrace?

XXVI
So faire, and thousand thousand times more faire,
She seemd, when she presented was to sight;
And was yclad, for heat of scorching aire,
All in a silken camus lylly whight,
Purfled upon with many a folded plight,
Which all above besprinckled was throughout
With golden aygulets, that glistred bright,
Like twinckling starres, and all the skirt about
Was hemd with golden fringe.

XXVII
Below her ham her weed did somewhat trayne,
And her streight legs most bravely were embayld
In gilden buskins of costly cordwayne,
All bard with golden bendes, which were entayld
With curious antickes, and full fayre aumayld:
Before, they fastned were under her knee
In a rich jewell, and therein entrayld
The ends of all their knots, that none might see
How they within their fouldings close enwrapped bee.

XXVIII
Like two faire marble pillours they were seene,
Which doe the temple of the gods support,
Whom all the people decke with girlands greene,
And honour in their festivall resort;
Those same with stately grace and princely port
She taught to tread, when she her selfe would grace,
But with the woody nymphes when she did sport,
Or when the flying libbard she did chace,
She could them nimbly move, and after fly apace.

XXIX

And in her hand a sharpe bore-speare she held,
And at her backe a bow and quiver gay,
Stuft with steele-headed dartes, wherewith she queld
The salvage beastes in her victorious play,
Knit with a golden bauldricke, which forelay
Athwart her snowy brest, and did divide
Her daintie paps; which, like young fruit in May,
Now little gan to swell, and being tide,
Through her thin weed their places only signifide.

XXX
Her yellow lockes, crisped like golden wyre,
About her shoulders weren loosely shed,
And when the winde emongst them did inspyre,
They waved like a penon wyde dispred,
And low behinde her backe were scattered:
And whether art it were, or heedelesse hap,
As through the flouring forrest rash she fled,
In her rude heares sweet flowres themselves did lap,
And flourishing fresh leaves and blossomes did enwrap.

XXXI
Such as Diana by the sandy shore
Of swift Eurotas, or on Cynthus greene,
Where all the nymphes have her unwares forlore,
Wandreth alone with bow and arrowes keene,
To seeke her game: or as that famous queene
Of Amazons, whom Pyrrhus did destroy,
The day that first of Priame she was seene,
Did shew her selfe in great triumphant joy,
To succour the weake state of sad afflicted Troy.

XXXII
Such when as hartlesse Trompart her did vew,
He was dismayed in his coward minde,
And doubted, whether he himselfe should shew,
Or fly away, or bide alone behinde:
Both feare and hope he in her face did finde,
When she at last, him spying, thus bespake:
'Hayle, groome! didst not thou see a bleeding hynde,
Whose right haunch earst my stedfast arrow strake?
If thou didst, tell me, that I may her overtake.'

XXXIII
Wherewith reviv'd, this answere forth he threw:
'O goddesse, (for such I thee take to bee;
For nether doth thy face terrestriall shew,
Nor voyce sound mortall) I avow to thee,
Such wounded beast as that I did not see,
Sith earst into this forrest wild I came.
But mote thy goodlyhed forgive it mee,

To weete which of the gods I shall thee name,
That unto thee dew worship I may rightly frame.'

XXXIV
To whom she thus— But ere her words ensewd,
Unto the bush her eye did suddein glaunce,
In which vaine Braggadocchio was mewd,
And saw it stirre: she lefte her percing launce,
And towards gan a deadly shafte advaunce,
In mind to marke the beast. At which sad stowre,
Trompart forth stept, to stay the mortall chaunce,
Out crying: 'O, what ever hevenly powre,
Or earthly wight thou be, withhold this deadly howre!

XXXV
'O stay thy hand! for yonder is no game
For thy fiers arrowes, them to exercize,
But loe! my lord, my liege, whose warlike name
Is far renowmd through many bold emprize;
And now in shade he shrowded yonder lies.'
She staid: with that he crauld out of his nest,
Forth creeping on his caitive hands and thies,
And standing stoutly up, his lofty crest
Did fiercely shake, and rowze, as comming late from rest.

XXXVI
As fearfull fowle, that long in secret cave
For dread of soring hauke her selfe hath hid,
Not caring how, her silly life to save,
She her gay painted plumes disorderid,
Seeing at last her selfe from daunger rid,
Peepes forth, and soone renews her native pride;
She gins her feathers fowle disfigured
Prowdly to prune, and sett on every side;
So shakes off shame, ne thinks how erst she did her hide.

XXXVII
So when her goodly visage he beheld,
He gan himselfe to vaunt; but when he vewd
Those deadly tooles which in her hand she held,
Soone into other fitts he was transmewd,
Till she to him her gracious speach renewd:
'All haile, sir knight, and well may thee befall,
As all the like, which honor have pursewd
Through deeds of armes and prowesse martiall!
All vertue merits praise, but such the most of all.'

XXXVIII
To whom he thus: 'O fairest under skie,
Trew be thy words, and worthy of thy praise,
That warlike feats doest highest glorifie.

Therein have I spent all my youthly daies,
And many battailes fought and many fraies
Throughout the world, wher so they might be found,
Endevoring my dreaded name to raise
Above the moone, that Fame may it resound
In her eternall tromp, with laurell girlond cround.

XXXIX
'But what art thou, O lady, which doest raunge
In this wilde forest, where no pleasure is,
And doest not it for joyous court exchaunge,
Emongst thine equall peres, where happy blis
And all delight does raigne, much more then this?
There thou maist love, and dearly loved be,
And swim in pleasure, which thou here doest mis;
There maist thou best be seene, and best maist see:
The wood is fit for beasts, the court is fitt for thee.'

XL
'Who so in pompe of prowd estate,' quoth she,
'Does swim, and bathes him selfe in courtly blis,
Does waste his dayes in darke obscuritee,
And in oblivion ever buried is:
Where ease abownds, yt's eath to doe amis:
But who his limbs with labours, and his mynd
Behaves with cares, cannot so easy mis.
Abroad in armes, at home in studious kynd,
Who seekes with painfull toile, shal Honor soonest fynd.

XLI
'In woods, in waves, in warres she wonts to dwell,
And wilbe found with perill and with paine;
Ne can the man, that moulds in ydle cell,
Unto her happy mansion attaine:
Before her gate High God did sweate ordaine,
And wakefull watches ever to abide:
But easy is the way, and passage plaine
To Pleasures pallace; it may soone be spide,
And day and night her dores to all stand open wide.

XLII
'In princes court—' The rest she would have sayd,
But that the foolish man, fild with delight
Of her sweete words, that all his sence dismayd,
And with her wondrous beauty ravisht quight,
Gan burne in filthy lust, and, leaping light,
Thought in his bastard armes her to embrace.
With that she, swarving backe, her javelin bright
Against him bent, and fiercely did menace:
So turned her about, and fled away apace.

XLIII
Which when the pesaunt saw, amazd he stood,
And grieved at her flight; yet durst he nott
Pursew her steps through wild unknowen wood;
Besides he feard her wrath, and threatned shott,
Whiles in the bush he lay, not yet forgott:
Ne car'd he greatly for her presence vayne,
But turning said to Trompart: 'What fowle blott
Is this to knight, that lady should agayne
Depart to woods untoucht, and leave so proud disdayne!'

XLIV
'Perdy,' said Trompart, 'lett her pas at will,
Least by her presence daunger mote befall.
For who can tell (and sure I feare it ill)
But that shee is some powre celestiall?
For whiles she spake, her great words did apall
My feeble corage, and my heart oppresse,
That yet I quake and tremble over all.'
'And I,' said Braggadocchio, 'thought no lesse,
When first I heard her horn sound with such ghastlinesse.

XLV
'For from my mothers wombe this grace I have
Me given by eternall destiny,
That earthly thing may not my corage brave
Dismay with feare, or cause on foote to flye,
But either hellish feends, or powres on hye:
Which was the cause, when earst that horne I heard,
Weening it had beene thunder in the skye,
I hid my selfe from it, as one affeard;
But when I other knew, my selfe I boldly reard.

XLVI
'But now, for feare of worse that may betide,
Let us soone hence depart.' They soone agree;
So to his steed he gott, and gan to ride,
As one unfitt therefore, that all might see
He had not trayned bene in chevalree.
Which well that valiaunt courser did discerne;
For he despisd to tread in dew degree,
But chaufd and fom'd, with corage fiers and sterne,
And to be easd of that base burden still did erne.

CANTO IV

**Guyon does Furor bind in chaines,
And stops Occasion:**

Delivers Phedon, and therefore
By Strife is rayld uppon.

I

In brave poursuitt of honorable deed,
There is I know not what great difference
Betweene the vulgar and the noble seed,
Which unto things of valorous pretence
Seemes to be borne by native influence;
As feates of armes, and love to entertaine;
But chiefly skill to ride seemes a science
Proper to gentle blood: some others faine
To menage steeds, as did this vaunter; but in vaine.

II

But he, the rightfull owner of that steede,
Who well could menage and subdew his pride,
The whiles on foot was forced for to yeed,
With that blacke palmer, his most trusty guide,
Who suffred not his wandring feete to slide;
But when strong passion, or weake fleshlinesse,
Would from the right way seeke to draw him wide,
He would, through temperaunce and stedfastnesse,
Teach him the weak to strengthen, and the strong suppresse.

III

It fortuned, forth faring on his way,
He saw from far, or seemed for to see,
Some troublous uprore or contentious fray,
Whereto he drew in hast, it to agree.
A mad man, or that feigned mad to bee,
Drew by the heare along upon the grownd
A handsom stripling with great crueltee,
Whom sore he bett, and gor'd with many a wownd,
That cheekes with teares, and sydes with blood did all abownd.

IV

And him behynd, a wicked hag did stalke,
In ragged robes and filthy disaray:
Her other leg was lame, that she no'te walke,
But on a staffe her feeble steps did stay:
Her lockes, that loathly were and hoarie gray,
Grew all afore, and loosly hong unrold,
But all behinde was bald, and worne away,
That none thereof could ever taken hold,
And eke her face ill favourd, full of wrinckles old.

V

And ever as she went, her toung did walke
In fowle reproch and termes of vile despight,

Provoking him, by her outrageous talke,
To heape more vengeance on that wretched wight;
Somtimes she raught him stones, wherwith to smite,
Sometimes her staffe, though it her one leg were,
Withouten which she could not goe upright;
Ne any evill meanes she did forbeare,
That might him move to wrath, and indignation reare.

VI
The noble Guyon, mov'd with great remorse,
Approching, first the hag did thrust away,
And after, adding more impetuous forse,
His mighty hands did on the madman lay,
And pluckt him backe; who, all on fire streight way,
Against him turning all his fell intent,
With beastly brutish rage gan him assay,
And smott, and bitt, and kickt, and scratcht, and rent,
And did he wist not what in his avengement.

VII
And sure he was a man of mickle might,
Had he had governaunce, it well to guyde:
But when the frantick fitt inflamd his spright,
His force was vaine, and strooke more often wyde
Then at the aymed marke which he had eyde:
And oft himselfe he chaunst to hurt unwares,
Whylest reason, blent through passion, nought descryde,
But as a blindfold bull at randon fares,
And where he hits, nought knowes, and whom he hurts, nought cares.

VIII
His rude assault and rugged handeling
Straunge seemed to the knight, that aye with foe
In fayre defence and goodly menaging
Of armes was wont to fight; yet nathemoe
Was he abashed now, not fighting so,
But, more enfierced through his currish play,
Him sternly grypt, and, hailing to and fro,
To overthrow him strongly did assay,
But overthrew him selfe unwares, and lower lay.

IX
And being downe, the villein sore did beate
And bruze with clownish fistes his manly face;
And eke the hag, with many a bitter threat,
Still cald upon to kill him in the place.
With whose reproch and odious menace
The knight emboyling in his haughtie hart,
Knitt all his forces, and gan soone unbrace
His grasping hold: so lightly did upstart,
And drew his deadly weapon, to maintaine his part.

X
Which when the palmer saw, he loudly cryde,
'Not so, O Guyon, never thinke that so
That monster can be maistred or destroyd:
He is not, ah! he is not such a foe,
As steele can wound, or strength can overthroe.
That same is Furor, cursed cruel wight,
That unto knighthood workes much shame and woe;
And that same hag, his aged mother, hight
Occasion, the roote of all wrath and despight.

XI
'With her, who so will raging Furor tame,
Must first begin, and well her amenage:
First her restraine from her reprochfull blame
And evill meanes, with which she doth enrage
Her frantick sonne, and kindles his corage;
Then, when she is withdrawne, or strong withstood,
It's eath his ydle fury to aswage,
And calme the tempest of his passion wood:
The bankes are overflowne, when stopped is the flood.'

XII
Therewith Sir Guyon left his first emprise,
And turning to that woman, fast her hent
By the hoare lockes that hong before her eyes,
And to the ground her threw: yet n' ould she stent
Her bitter rayling and foule revilement,
But still provokt her sonne to wreake her still torment,
And catching hold of her ungratious tonge,
Thereon an yron lock did fasten firme and strong.

XIII
Then whenas use of speach was from her reft,
With her two crooked handes she signes did make,
And beckned him, the last help she had left:
But he that last left helpe away did take,
And both her handes fast bound unto a stake,
That she note stirre. Then gan her sonne to flye
Full fast away, and did her quite forsake;
But Guyon after him in hast did hye,
And soone him overtooke in sad perplexitye.

XIV
In his strong armes he stifly him embraste,
Who, him gainstriving, nought at all prevaild:
For all his power was utterly defaste,
And furious fitts at earst quite weren quaild:
Oft he re'nforst, and oft his forces fayld,
Yet yield he would not, nor his rancor slack.

Then him to ground he cast, and rudely hayld,
And both his hands fast bound behind his backe,
And both his feet in fetters to an yron rack.

XV
With hundred yron chaines he did him bind,
And hundred knots, that did him sore constraine:
Yet his great yron teeth he still did grind,
And grimly gnash, threatning revenge in vaine:
His burning eyen, whom bloody strakes did staine,
Stared full wide, and threw forth sparkes of fyre,
And more for ranck despight then for great paine,
Shakt his long locks, colourd like copper-wyre,
And bitt his tawny beard to shew his raging yre.

XVI
Thus whenas Guyon Furor had captivd,
Turning about he saw that wretched squyre,
Whom that mad man of life nigh late deprivd,
Lying on ground, all soild with blood and myre:
Whom whenas he perceived to respyre,
He gan to comfort, and his woundes to dresse.
Being at last recured, he gan inquyre,
What hard mishap him brought to such distresse,
And made that caytives thrall, the thrall of wretchednesse.

XVII
With hart then throbbing, and with watry eyes,
'Fayre sir,' quoth he, 'what man can shun the hap,
That hidden lyes unwares him to surpryse?
Misfortune waites advantage to entrap
The man most wary in her whelming lap.
So me, weake wretch, of many weakest one,
Unweeting, and unware of such mishap,
She brought to mischiefe through occasion,
Where this same wicked villein did me light upon.

XVIII
'It was a faithlesse squire, that was the sourse
Of all my sorrow, and of these sad teares,
With whom from tender dug of commune nourse
Attonce I was upbrought, and eft, when yeares
More rype us reason lent to chose our peares,
Our selves in league of vowed love wee knitt:
In which we long time, without gealous feares
Or faultie thoughts, contynewd, as was fitt;
And, for my part I vow, dissembled not a whitt.

XIX
'It was my fortune, commune to that age,
To love a lady fayre of great degree,

The which was borne of noble parentage,
And set in highest seat of dignitee,
Yet seemd no lesse to love then loved to bee:
Long I her serv'd, and found her faithfull still,
Ne ever thing could cause us disagree:
Love, that two harts makes one, makes eke one will:
Each strove to please, and others pleasure to fulfill.

XX
'My friend, hight Philemon, I did partake
Of all my love and all my privitie;
Who greatly joyous seemed for my sake,
And gratious to that lady, as to mee;
Ne ever wight, that mote so welcome bee
As he to her, withouten blott or blame,
Ne ever thing, that she could thinke or see,
But unto him she would impart the same:
O wretched man, that would abuse so gentle dame!

XXI
'At last such grace I found, and meanes I wrought,
That I that lady to my spouse had wonne;
Accord of friendes, consent of parents sought,
Affyaunce made, my happinesse begonne,
There wanted nought but few rites to be donne,
Which mariage make: that day too farre did seeme:
Most joyous man on whom the shining sunne
Did shew his face, my selfe I did esteeme,
And that my falser friend did no lesse joyous deeme.

XXII
'But ear that wished day his beame disclosd,
He, either envying my toward good,
Or of himselfe to treason ill disposd,
One day unto me came in friendly mood,
And told for secret, how he understood,
That lady, whom I had to me assynd,
Had both distaind her honorable blood,
And eke the faith which she to me did bynd;
And therfore wisht me stay, till I more truth should fynd.

XXIII
'The gnawing anguish and sharp gelosy,
Which his sad speach infixed in my brest,
Ranckled so sore, and festred inwardly,
That my engreeved mind could find no rest,
Till that the truth thereof I did out wrest;
And him besought, by that same sacred band
Betwixt us both, to counsell me the best.
He then with solemne oath and plighted hand
Assurd, ere long the truth to let me understand.

XXIV
'Ere long with like againe he boorded mee,
Saying, he now had boulted all the floure,
And that it was a groome of base degree,
Which of my love was partener paramoure:
Who used in a darkesome inner bowre
Her oft to meete: which better to approve,
He promised to bring me at that howre,
When I should see that would me nearer move,
And drive me to withdraw my blind abused love.

XXV
'This gracelesse man, for furtherance of his guile,
Did court the handmayd of my lady deare,
Who, glad t' embosome his affection vile,
Did all she might, more pleasing to appeare.
One day, to worke her to his will more neare,
He woo'd her thus: "Pryene," (so she hight)
"What great despight doth Fortune to thee beare,
Thus lowly to abase thy beautie bright,
That it should not deface all others lesser light?

XXVI
'"But if she had her least helpe to thee lent,
T' adorne thy forme according thy desart,
Their blazing pride thou wouldest soone have blent,
And staynd their prayses with thy least good part;
Ne should faire Claribell with all her art,
Though she thy lady be, approch thee neare:
For proofe thereof, this evening, as thou art,
Aray thy selfe in her most gorgeous geare,
That I may more delight in thy embracement deare."

XXVII
'The mayden, proud through praise and mad through love,
Him hearkned to, and soone her selfe arayd,
The whiles to me the treachour did remove
His craftie engin, and, as he had sayd,
Me leading, in a secret corner layd,
The sad spectatour of my tragedie;
Where left, he went, and his owne false part playd,
Disguised like that groome of base degree,
Whom he had feignd th' abuser of my love to bee.

XXVIII
'Eftsoones he came unto th' appointed place,
And with him brought Pryene, rich arayd,
In Claribellaes clothes. Her proper face
I not descerned in that darkesome shade,
But weend it was my love with whom he playd.

Ah God! what horrour and tormenting griefe
My hart, my handes, mine eyes, and all assayd!
Me liefer were ten thousand deathes priefe,
Then wounde of gealous worme, and shame of such repriefe.

XXIX

'I home retourning, fraught with fowle despight,
And chawing vengeaunce all the way I went,
Soone as my loathed love appeard in sight,
With wrathfull hand I slew her innocent;
That after soone I dearely did lament:
For when the cause of that outrageous deede
Demaunded, I made plaine and evident,
Her faultie handmayd, which that bale did breede,
Confest how Philemon her wrought to chaunge her weede.

XXX

'Which when I heard, with horrible affright
And hellish fury all enragd, I sought
Upon my selfe that vengeable despight
To punish: yet it better first I thought,
To wreake my wrath on him that first it wrought.
To Philemon, false faytour Philemon,
I cast to pay that I so dearely bought:
Of deadly drugs I gave him drinke anon,
And washt away his guilt with guilty potion.

XXXI

'Thus heaping crime on crime, and griefe on griefe,
To loose of love adjoyning losse of frend,
I meant to purge both with a third mischiefe,
And in my woes beginner it to end.
That was Pryene; she did first offend,
She last should smart: with which cruell intent,
When I at her my murdrous blade did bend,
She fled away with ghastly dreriment,
And I, poursewing my fell purpose, after went.

XXXII

'Feare gave her winges, and rage enforst my flight:
Through woods and plaines so long I did her chace,
Till this mad man, whom your victorious might
Hath now fast bound, me met in middle space:
As I her, so he me poursewd apace,
And shortly overtooke: I, breathing yre,
Sore chauffed at my stay in such a cace,
And with my heat kindled his cruell fyre;
Which kindled once, his mother did more rage inspyre.

XXXIII

'Betwixt them both, they have me doen to dye,

Through wounds, and strokes, and stubborne handeling,
That death were better then such agony
As griefe and fury unto me did bring;
Of which in me yet stickes the mortall sting,
That during life will never be appeasd.'
When he thus ended had his sorrowing,
Said Guyon: 'Squyre, sore have ye beene diseasd;
But all your hurts may soone through temperance be easd.'

XXXIV
Then gan the palmer thus: 'Most wretched man,
That to affections does the bridle lend!
In their beginning they are weake and wan,
But soone through suff'rance growe to fearefull end.
Whiles they are weake, betimes with them contend:
For when they once to perfect strength do grow,
Strong warres they make, and cruell battry bend
Gainst fort of reason, it to overthrow:
Wrath, gelosy, griefe, love this squyre have laide thus low.

XXXV
'Wrath, gealosie, griefe, love do thus expell:
Wrath is a fire, and gealosie a weede,
Griefe is a flood, and love a monster fell;
The fire of sparkes, the weede of little seede,
The flood of drops, the monster filth did breede:
But sparks, seed, drops, and filth do thus delay;
The sparks soone quench, the springing seed outweed,
The drops dry up, and filth wipe cleane away:
So shall wrath, gealosy, griefe, love die and decay.'

XXXVI
'Unlucky squire,' saide Guyon, 'sith thou hast
Falne into mischiefe through intemperaunce,
Henceforth take heede of that thou now hast past,
And guyde thy waies with warie governaunce,
Least worse betide thee by some later chaunce.
But read how art thou nam'd, and of what kin.'
'Phedon I hight,' quoth he, 'and do advaunce
Mine auncestry from famous Coradin,
Who first to rayse our house to honour did begin.'

XXXVII
Thus as he spake, lo! far away they spyde
A varlet ronning towardes hastily,
Whose flying feet so fast their way applyde,
That round about a cloud of dust did fly,
Which, mingled all with sweate, did dim his eye.
He soone approched, panting, breathlesse, whot,
And all so soyld, that none could him descry.
His countenaunce was bold, and bashed not

For Guyons lookes, but scornefull eyglaunce at him shot.

XXXVIII
Behind his backe he bore a brasen shield,
On which was drawen faire, in colours fit,
A flaming fire in midst of bloody field,
And round about the wreath this word was writ,
Burnt I doe burne. Right well beseemed it
To be the shield of some redoubted knight:
And in his hand two dartes exceeding flit
And deadly sharp he held, whose heads were dight
In poyson and in blood of malice and despight.

XXXIX
When he in presence came, to Guyon first
He boldly spake: 'Sir knight, if knight thou bee,
Abandon this forestalled place at erst,
For feare of further harme, I counsell thee;
Or bide the chaunce at thine owne jeopardee.'
The knight at his great boldnesse wondered,
And though he scornd his ydle vanitee,
Yet mildly him to purpose answered;
For not to grow of nought he it conjectured.

XL
'Varlet, this place most dew to me I deeme,
Yielded by him that held it forcibly.
But whence shold come that harme, which thou dost seeme
To threat to him that mindes his chaunce t' abye?'
'Perdy,' sayd he, 'here comes, and is hard by,
A knight of wondrous powre and great assay,
That never yet encountred enemy,
But did him deadly daunt, or fowle dismay;
Ne thou for better hope, if thou his presence stay.'

XLI
'How hight he then,' sayd Guyon, 'and from whence?'
'Pyrochles is his name, renowmed farre
For his bold feates and hardy confidence,
Full oft approvd in many a cruell warre;
The brother of Cymochles, both which arre
The sonnes of old Acrates and Despight,
Acrates, sonne of Phlegeton and Jarre;
But Phlegeton is sonne of Herebus and Night;
But Herebus sonne of Aeternitie is hight.

XLII
'So from immortall race he does proceede,
That mortall hands may not withstand his might,
Drad for his derring doe and bloody deed;
For all in blood and spoile is his delight.

His am I Atin, his in wrong and right,
That matter make for him to worke upon,
And stirre him up to strife and cruell fight.
Fly therefore, fly this fearfull stead anon,
Least thy foolhardize worke thy sad confusion.'

XLIII
'His be that care, whom most it doth concerne,'
Sayd he: 'but whether with such hasty flight
Art thou now bownd? for well mote I discerne
Great cause, that carries thee so swifte and light.'
'My lord,' quoth he, 'me sent, and streight behight
To seeke Occasion, where so she bee:
For he is all disposd to bloody fight,
And breathes out wrath and hainous crueltee:
Hard is his hap, that first fals in his jeopardee.'

XLIV
'Mad man,' said then the palmer, 'that does seeke
Occasion to wrath, and cause of strife!
Shee comes unsought, and shonned followes eke.
Happy who can abstaine, when Rancor rife
Kindles revenge, and threats his rusty knife:
Woe never wants, where every cause is caught,
And rash Occasion makes unquiet life.'
'Then loe! wher bound she sits, whom thou hast sought,'
Said Guyon: 'let that message to thy lord be brought.'

XLV
That when the varlett heard and saw, streight way
He wexed wondrous wroth, and said: 'Vile knight,
That knights and knighthood doest with shame upbray,
And shewst th' ensample of thy childishe might,
With silly weake old woman thus to fight!
Great glory and gay spoile sure hast thou gott,
And stoutly prov'd thy puissaunce here in sight.
That shall Pyrochles well requite, I wott,
And with thy blood abolish so reprochfull blott.'

XLVI
With that, one of his thrillant darts he threw,
Headed with yre and vengeable despight:
The quivering steele his aymed end wel knew,
And to his brest it selfe intended right.
But he was wary, and, ere it empight
In the meant marke, advaunst his shield atweene,
On which it seizing, no way enter might,
But backe rebownding left the forckhead keene:
Eftsoones he fled away, and might no where be seene.

CANTO V

Pyrochles does with Guyon fight,
And Furors chayne unbinds;
Of whom sore hurt, for his revenge
Attin Cymochles finds.

I

Who ever doth to temperaunce apply
His stedfast life, and all his actions frame,
Trust me, shal find no greater enimy,
Then stubborne perturbation, to the same;
To which right wel the wise doe give that name;
For it the goodly peace of staied mindes
Does overthrow, and troublous warre proclame:
His owne woes author, who so bound it findes,
As did Pyrochles, and it wilfully unbindes.

II

After that varlets flight, it was not long,
Ere on the plaine fast pricking Guyon spide
One in bright armes embatteiled full strong,
That as the sunny beames doe glaunce and glide
Upon the trembling wave, so shined bright,
And round about him threw forth sparkling fire,
That seemd him to enflame on every side:
His steed was bloody red, and fomed yre,
When with the maistring spur he did him roughly stire.

III

Approching nigh, he never staid to greete,
Ne chaffar words, prowd corage to provoke,
But prickt so fiers, that underneath his feete
The smouldring dust did rownd about him smoke,
Both horse and man nigh able for to choke;
And fayrly couching his steele headed speare,
Him first saluted with a sturdy stroke:
It booted nought Sir Guyon, comming neare,
To thincke such hideous puissaunce on foot to beare;

IV

But lightly shunned it, and passing by,
With his bright blade did smite at him so fell,
That the sharpe steele, arriving forcibly
On his broad shield, bitt not, but glauncing fell
On his horse necke before the quilted sell,
And from the head the body sundred quight.
So him, dismounted low, he did compell

On foot with him to matchen equall fight;
The truncked beast, fast bleeding, did him fowly dight.

V
Sore bruzed with the fall, he slow uprose,
And all enraged, thus him loudly shent:
'Disleall knight, whose coward corage chose
To weake it selfe on beast all innocent,
And shund the market at which it should be ment!
Therby thine armes seem strong, but manhood frayl:
So hast thou oft with guile thine honor blent;
But litle may such guile thee now avayl,
If wonted force and fortune doe not much me fayl.'

VI
With that he drew his flaming sword, and strooke
At him so fiercely, that the upper marge
Of his sevenfolded shield away it tooke,
And glauncing on his helmet, made a large
And open gash therein: were not his targe,
That broke the violence of his intent,
The weary sowle from thence it would discharge:
Nathelesse so sore a buff to him it lent,
That made him reele, and to his brest his bever bent.

VII
Exceeding wroth was Guyon at that blow,
And much ashamd that stroke of living arme
Should him dismay, and make him stoup so low,
Though otherwise it did him litle harme:
Tho, hurling high his yron braced arme,
He smote so manly on his shoulder plate,
That all his left side it did quite disarme;
Yet there the steele stayd not, but inly bate
Deepe in his flesh, and opened wide a red floodgate.

VIII
Deadly dismayd with horror of that dint
Pyrochles was, and grieved eke entyre;
Yet nathemore did it his fury stint,
But added flame unto his former fire,
That welnigh molt his hart in raging yre;
Ne thenceforth his approved skill, to ward,
Or strike, or hurtle rownd in warlike gyre,
Remembred he, ne car'd for his saufgard,
But rudely rag'd, and like a cruel tygre far'd.

IX
He hewd, and lasht, and foynd, and thondred blowes,
And every way did seeke into his life;
Ne plate, ne male could ward so mighty throwes,

But yeilded passage to his cruell knife.
But Guyon, in the heat of all his strife,
Was wary wise, and closely did awayt
Avauntage, whilest his foe did rage most rife:
Sometimes a thwart, sometimes he strook him strayt,
And falsed oft his blowes, t' illude him with such bayt.

X

Like as a lyon, whose imperiall powre
A prowd rebellious unicorne defyes,
T' avoide the rash assault and wrathfull stowre
Of his fiers foe, him to a tree applyes,
And when him ronning in full course he spyes,
He slips aside; the whiles that furious beast
His precious horne, sought of his enimyes,
Strikes in the stocke, ne thence can be releast,
But to the mighty victor yields a bounteous feast.

XI

With such faire sleight him Guyon often fayld,
Till at the last all breathlesse, weary, faint
Him spying, with fresh onsett he assayld,
And kindling new his corage seeming queint,
Strooke him so hugely, that through great constraint
He made him stoup perforce unto his knee,
And doe unwilling worship to the saint,
That on his shield depainted he did see:
Such homage till that instant never learned hee.

XII

Whom Guyon seeing stoup, poursewed fast
The present offer of faire victory,
And soone his dreadfull blade about he cast,
Wherewith he smote his haughty crest so hye,
That streight on grownd made him full low to lye;
Then on his brest his victor foote he thrust:
With that he cryde: 'Mercy! doe me not dye,
Ne deeme thy force by Fortunes doome unjust,
That hath (maugre her spight!) thus low me laid in dust.'

XIII

Eftsoones his cruel hand Sir Guyon stayd,
Tempring the passion with advizement slow,
And maistring might on enimy dismayd;
For th' equall die of warre he well did know:
Then to him said: 'Live, and alleagaunce owe
To him that gives thee life and liberty,
And henceforth by this daies ensample trow,
That hasty wroth, and heedlesse hazardry,
Doe breede repentaunce late, and lasting infamy.'

XIV
So up he let him rise; who, with grim looke
And count'naunce sterne upstanding, gan to grind
His grated teeth for great disdeigne, and shooke
His sandy lockes, long hanging downe behind,
Knotted in blood and dust, for griefe of mind,
That he in ods of armes was conquered;
Yet in himselfe some comfort he did find,
That him so noble knight had maystered,
Whose bounty more then might, yet both, he wondered.

XV
Which Guyon marking said: 'Be nought agriev'd,
Sir knight, that thus ye now subdewed arre:
Was never man, who most conquestes atchiev'd,
But sometimes had the worse, and lost by warre,
Yet shortly gaynd that losse exceeded farre:
Losse is no shame, nor to bee lesse then foe,
But to bee lesser then himselfe doth marre
Both loosers lott, and victours prayse alsoe:
Vaine others overthrowes who selfe doth overthrow.

XVI
'Fly, O Pyrochles, fly the dreadfull warre,
That in thy selfe thy lesser partes doe move,
Outrageous anger, and woe working jarre,
Direfull impatience, and hartmurdring love;
Those, those thy foes, those warriours far remove,
Which thee to endlesse bale captived lead.
But sith in might thou didst my mercy prove,
Of courtesie to mee the cause aread,
That thee against me drew with so impetuous dread.'

XVII
'Dreadlesse,' said he, 'that shall I soone declare:
It was complaind that thou hadst done great tort
Unto an aged woman, poore and bare,
And thralled her in chaines with strong effort,
Voide of all succour and needfull comfort:
That ill beseemes thee, such as I thee see,
To worke such shame. Therefore I thee exhort
To chaunge thy will, and set Occasion free,
And to her captive sonne yield his first libertee.'

XVIII
Thereat Sir Guyon smylde: 'And is that all,'
Said he, 'that thee so sore displeased hath?
Great mercy sure, for to enlarge a thrall,
Whose freedom shall thee turne to greatest scath!
Nath'lesse now quench thy whott emboyling wrath:
Loe! there they bee; to thee I yield them free.'

Thereat he wondrous glad, out of the path
Did lightly leape, where he them bound did see,
And gan to breake the bands of their captivitee.

XIX

Soone as Occasion felt her selfe untyde,
Before her sonne could well assoyled bee,
She to her use returnd, and streight defyde
Both Guyon and Pyrochles: th' one (said shee)
Bycause he wonne; the other because hee
Was wonne: so matter did she make of nought,
To stirre up strife, and do them disagree:
But soone as Furor was enlargd, she sought
To kindle his quencht fyre, and thousand causes wrought.

XX

It was not long ere she inflam'd him so,
That he would algates with Pyrochles fight,
And his redeemer chalengd for his foe,
Because he had not well mainteind his right,
But yielded had to that same straunger knight:
Now gan Pyrochles wex as wood as hee,
And him affronted with impatient might:
So both together fiers engrasped bee,
Whyles Guyon, standing by, their uncouth strife does see.

XXI

Him all that while Occasion did provoke
Against Pyrochles, and new matter fram'd
Upon the old, him stirring to bee wroke
Of his late wronges, in which she oft him blam'd
For suffering such abuse as knighthood sham'd,
And him dishabled quyte. But he was wise,
Ne would with vaine occasions be inflam'd;
Yet others she more urgent did devise;
Yet nothing could him to impatience entise.

XXII

Their fell contention still increased more,
And more thereby increased Furors might,
That he his foe has hurt, and wounded sore,
And him in blood and durt deformed quight.
His mother eke, more to augment his spight,
Now brought to him a flaming fyer brond,
Which she in Stygian lake, ay burning bright,
Had kindled: that she gave into his hond,
That, armd with fire, more hardly he mote him withstond.

XXIII

Tho gan that villein wex so fiers and strong,
That nothing might sustaine his furious forse:

He cast him downe to ground, and all along
Drew him through durt and myre without remorse,
And fowly battered his comely corse,
That Guyon much disdeignd so loathly sight.
At last he was compeld to cry perforse,
'Help, O Sir Guyon! helpe, most noble knight,
To ridd a wretched man from handes of hellish wight!'

XXIV
The knight was greatly moved at his playnt,
And gan him dight to succour his distresse,
Till that the palmer, by his grave restraynt,
Him stayd from yielding pitifull redresse,
And said: 'Deare sonne, thy causelesse ruth represse,
Ne let thy stout hart melt in pitty vayne:
He that his sorow sought through wilfulnesse,
And his foe fettred would release agayne,
Deserves to taste his follies fruit, repented payne.'

XXV
Guyon obayd: so him away he drew
From needlesse trouble of renewing fight
Already fought, his voyage to poursew.
But rash Pyrochles varlett, Atin hight,
When late he saw his lord in heavie plight,
Under Sir Guyons puissaunt stroke to fall,
Him deeming dead, as then he seemd in sight,
Fledd fast away, to tell his funerall
Unto his brother, whom Cymochles men did call.

XXVI
He was a man of rare redoubted might,
Famous throughout the world for warlike prayse,
And glorious spoiles, purchast in perilous fight:
Full many doughtie knightes he in his dayes
Had doen to death, subdewde in equall frayes,
Whose carkases, for terrour of his name,
Of fowles and beastes he made the piteous prayes,
And hong their conquerd armes for more defame
On gallow trees, in honour of his dearest dame.

XXVII
His dearest dame is that enchaunteresse,
The vyle Acrasia, that with vaine delightes,
And ydle pleasures in her Bowre of Blisse,
Does charme her lovers, and the feeble sprightes
Can call out of the bodies of fraile wightes;
Whom then she does trasforme to monstrous hewes,
And horribly misshapes with ugly sightes,
Captiv'd eternally in yron mewes,
And darksom dens, where Titan his face never shewes.

XXVIII
There Atin fownd Cymochles sojourning,
To serve his lemans love: for he by kynd
Was given all to lust and loose living,
When ever his fiers handes he free mote fynd:
And now he has pourd out his ydle mynd
In daintie delices and lavish joyes,
Having his warlike weapons cast behynd,
And flowes in pleasures and vaine pleasing toyes,
Mingled emongst loose ladies and lascivious boyes.

XXIX
And over him, Art, stryving to compayre
With Nature, did an arber greene dispred,
Framed of wanton yvie, flouring fayre,
Through which the fragrant eglantine did spred
His prickling armes, entrayld with roses red,
Which daintie odours round about them threw;
And all within with flowres was garnished,
That, when myld Zephyrus emongst them blew,
Did breath out bounteous smels, and painted colors shew.

XXX
And fast beside, there trickled softly downe
A gentle streame, whose murmuring wave did play
Emongst the pumy stones, and made a sowne,
To lull him soft a sleepe, that by it lay:
The wearie traveiler, wandring that way,
Therein did often quench his thristy heat,
And then by it his wearie limbes display,
Whiles creeping slomber made him to forget
His former payne, and wypt away his toilsom sweat.

XXXI
And on the other syde a pleasaunt grove
Was shott up high, full of the stately tree
That dedicated is t' Olympick Jove,
And to his sonne Alcides, whenas hee
Gaynd in Nemea goodly victoree:
Therein the mery birdes of every sorte
Chaunted alowd their chearefull harmonee,
And made emongst them selves a sweete consort,
That quickned the dull spright with musicall comfort.

XXXII
There he him found all carelesly displaid,
In secrete shadow from the sunny ray,
On a sweet bed of lillies softly laid,
Amidst a flock of damzelles fresh and gay,
That rownd about him dissolute did play

Their wanton follies and light meriment;
Every of which did loosely disaray
Her upper partes of meet habiliments,
And shewd them naked, deckt with many ornaments.

XXXIII
And every of them strove, with most delights
Him to aggrate, and greatest pleasures shew;
Some framd faire lookes, glancing like evening lights,
Others sweet wordes, dropping like honny dew;
Some bathed kisses, and did soft embrew
The sugred licour through his melting lips:
One boastes her beautie, and does yield to vew
Her dainty limbes above her tender hips;
Another her out boastes, and all for tryall strips.

XXXIV
He, like an adder lurking in the weedes,
His wandring thought in deepe desire does steepe,
And his frayle eye with spoyle of beauty feedes:
Sometimes he falsely faines himselfe to sleepe,
Whiles through their lids his wanton eies do peepe,
To steale a snatch of amorous conceipt,
Whereby close fire into his heart does creepe:
So' he them deceives, deceivd in his deceipt,
Made dronke with drugs of deare voluptuous receipt.

XXXV
Attin, arriving there, when him he spyde
Thus in still waves of deepe delight to wade,
Fiercely approching, to him lowdly cryde,
'Cymochles! oh! no, but Cymochles shade,
In which that manly person late did fade!
What is become of great Acrates sonne?
Or where hath he hong up his mortall blade,
That hath so many haughty conquests wonne?
Is all his force forlorne, and all his glory donne?'

XXXVI
Then pricking him with his sharp-pointed dart,
He saide: 'Up, up! thou womanish weake knight,
That here in ladies lap entombed art,
Unmindfull of thy praise and prowest might,
And weetlesse eke of lately wrought despight,
Whiles sad Pyrochles lies on sencelesse ground,
And groneth out his utmost grudging spright,
Through many a stroke, and many a streaming wound,
Calling thy help in vaine, that here in joyes art dround.'

XXXVII
Suddeinly out of his delightfull dreame

The man awoke, and would have questiond more;
But he would not endure that wofull theame
For to dilate at large, but urged sore,
With percing wordes and pittifull implore,
Him hasty to arise. As one affright
With hellish feends, or Furies mad uprore,
He then uprose, inflamd with fell despight,
And called for his armes; for he would algates fight.

XXXVIII
They bene ybrought; he quickly does him dight,
And, lightly mounted, passeth on his way;
Ne ladies loves, ne sweete entreaties might
Appease his heat, or hastie passage stay;
For he has vowd to beene avengd that day
(That day it selfe him seemed all too long)
On him that did Pyrochles deare dismay:
So proudly pricketh on his courser strong,
And Attin ay him pricks with spurs of shame and wrong.

CANTO VI

Guyon is of Immodest Merth
Led into loose desyre;
Fights with Cymochles, whiles his
Brother burnes in furious fyre.

I
A harder lesson to learne continence
In joyous pleasure then in grievous paine:
For sweetnesse doth allure the weaker sence
So strongly, that uneathes it can refraine
From that which feeble nature covets faine;
But griefe and wrath, that be her enemies,
And foes of life, she better can restraine;
Yet Vertue vauntes in both her victories,
And Guyon in them all shewes goodly maysteries.

II
Whom bold Cymochles traveiling to finde,
With cruell purpose bent to wreake on him
The wrath which Atin kindled in his mind,
Came to a river, by whose utmost brim
Wayting to passe, he saw whereas did swim
Along the shore, as swift as glaunce of eye,
A litle gondelay, bedecked trim
With boughes and arbours woven cunningly,

That like a litle forrest seemed outwardly.

III
And therein sate a lady fresh and fayre,
Making sweete solace to herselfe alone;
Sometimes she song, as lowd as larke in ayre,
Sometimes she laught, that nigh her breth was gone,
Yet was there not with her else any one,
That might to her move cause of meriment:
Matter of merth enough, though there were none,
She could devise, and thousand waies invent,
To feede her foolish humour and vaine jolliment.

IV
Which when far of Cymochles heard and saw,
He lowdly cald to such as were abord,
The little barke unto the shore to draw,
And him to ferry over that deepe ford.
The merry mariner unto his word
Soone hearkned, and her painted bote streightway
Turnd to the shore, where that same warlike lord
She in receiv'd; but Atin by no way
She would admit, albe the knight her much did pray.

V
Eftsoones her shallow ship away did slide,
More swift then swallow sheres the liquid skye,
Withouten oare or pilot it to guide,
Or winged canvas with the wind to fly:
Onely she turnd a pin, and by and by
It cut away upon the yielding wave;
Ne cared she her course for to apply:
For it was taught the way which she would have,
And both from rocks and flats it selfe could wisely save.

VI
And all the way, the wanton damsell found
New merth, her passenger to entertaine:
For she in pleasaunt purpose did abound,
And greatly joyed merry tales to faine,
Of which a store-house did with her remaine:
Yet seemed, nothing well they her became;
For all her wordes she drownd with laughter vaine,
And wanted grace in utt'ring of the same,
That turned all her pleasaunce to a scoffing game.

VII
And other whiles vaine toyes she would devize,
As her fantasticke wit did most delight:
Sometimes her head she fondly would aguize
With gaudy girlonds, or fresh flowrets dight

About her necke, or rings of rushes plight;
Sometimes, to do him laugh, she would assay
To laugh at shaking of the leaves light,
Or to behold the water worke and play
About her little frigot, therein making way.

VIII
Her light behaviour and loose dalliaunce
Gave wondrous great contentment to the knight,
That of his way he had no sovenaunce,
Nor care of vow'd revenge and cruell fight,
But to weake wench did yield his martiall might:
So easie was, to quench his flamed minde
With one sweete drop of sensuall delight;
So easie is, t' appease the stormy winde
Of malice in the calme of pleasaunt womankind.

IX
Diverse discourses in their way they spent,
Mongst which Cymochles of her questioned,
Both what she was, and what that usage ment,
Which in her cott she daily practized.
'Vaine man!' saide she, 'that wouldest be reckoned
A straunger in thy home, and ignoraunt
Of Phædria (for so my name is red)
Of Phædria, thine owne fellow servaunt;
For thou to serve Acrasia thy selfe doest vaunt.

X
'In this wide inland sea, that hight by name
The Idle Lake, my wandring ship I row,
That knowes her port, and thether sayles by ayme;
Ne care, ne feare I, how the wind do blow,
Or whether swift I wend, or whether slow:
Both slow and swift a like do serve my tourne:
Ne swelling Neptune, ne lowd thundring Jove
Can chaunge my cheare, or make me ever mourne:
My little boat can safely passe this perilous bourne.'

XI
Whiles thus she talked, and whiles thus she toyd,
They were far past the passage which he spake,
And come unto an island, waste and voyd,
That floted in the midst of that great lake.
There her small gondelay her port did make,
And that gay payre issewing on the shore
Disburdned her. Their way they forward take
Into the land, that lay them faire before,
Whose pleasaunce she him shewd, and plentifull great store.

XII

It was a chosen plott of fertile land,
Emongst wide waves sett, like a litle nest,
As if it had by Natures cunning hand
Bene choycely picked out from all the rest,
And laid forth for ensample of the best:
No dainty flowre or herbe, that growes on grownd,
No arborett with painted blossomes drest,
And smelling sweete, but there it might be fownd
To bud out faire, and her sweete smels throwe al arownd.

XIII
No tree, whose braunches did not bravely spring;
No braunch, whereon a fine bird did not sitt;
No bird, but did her shrill notes sweetely sing;
No song, but did containe a lovely ditt:
Trees, braunches, birds, and songs were framed fitt
For to allure fraile mind to carelesse ease.
Carelesse the man soone woxe, and his weake witt
Was overcome of thing that did him please;
So pleased, did his wrathfull purpose faire appease.

XIV
Thus when shee had his eyes and sences fed
With false delights, and fild with pleasures vayn,
Into a shady dale she soft him led,
And laid him downe upon a grassy playn;
And her sweete selfe without dread or disdayn
She sett beside, laying his head disarmd
In her loose lap, it softly to sustayn,
Where soone he slumbred, fearing not be harmd,
The whiles with a love lay she thus him sweetly charmd:

XV
'Behold, O man, that toilesome paines doest take,
The flowrs, the fields, and all that pleasaunt growes,
How they them selves doe thine ensample make,
Whiles nothing envious Nature them forth throwes
Out of her fruitfull lap; how no man knowes,
They spring, they bud, they blossome fresh and faire,
And decke the world with their rich pompous showes;
Yet no man for them taketh paines or care,
Yet no man to them can his carefull paines compare.

XVI
'The lilly, lady of the flowring field,
The flowre deluce, her lovely paramoure,
Bid thee to them thy fruitlesse labors yield,
And soone leave off this toylsome weary stoure:
Loe, loe, how brave she decks her bounteous boure,
With silkin curtens and gold coverletts,
Therein to shrowd her sumptuous belamoure!

Yet nether spinnes nor cards, ne cares nor fretts,
But to her mother Nature all her care she letts.

XVII
'Why then doest thou, O man, that of them all
Art lord, and eke of Nature soveraine,
Wilfully make thy selfe a wretched thrall,
And waste thy joyous howres in needelesse paine,
Seeking for daunger and adventures vaine?
What bootes it al to have, and nothing use?
Who shall him rew, that swimming in the maine
Will die for thrist, and water doth refuse?
Refuse such fruitlesse toile, and present pleasures chuse.'

XVIII
By this she had him lulled fast a sleepe,
That of no worldly thing he care did take;
Then she with liquors strong his eies did steepe,
That nothing should him hastily awake:
So she him lefte, and did her selfe betake
Unto her boat again, with which she clefte
The slouthfull wave of that great griesy lake;
Soone shee that island far behind her lefte,
And now is come to that same place, where first she wefte.

XIX
By this time was the worthy Guyon brought
Unto the other side of that wide strond,
Where she was rowing, and for passage sought:
Him needed not long call; shee soone to hond
Her ferry brought, where him she byding fond
With his sad guide: him selfe she tooke a boord,
But the blacke palmer suffred still to stond,
Ne would for price or prayers once affoord,
To ferry that old man over the perlous foord.

XX
Guyon was loath to leave his guide behind,
Yet, being entred, might not backe retyre;
For the flitt barke, obaying to her mind,
Forth launched quickly, as she did desire,
Ne gave him leave to bid that aged sire
Adieu, but nimbly ran her wonted course
Through the dull billowes thicke as troubled mire,
Whom nether wind out of their seat could forse,
Nor timely tides did drive out of their sluggish sourse.

XXI
And by the way, as was her wonted guize,
Her mery fitt shee freshly gan to reare,
And did of joy and jollity devize,

Her selfe to cherish, and her guest to cheare.
The knight was courteous, and did not forbeare
Her honest merth and pleasaunce to partake;
But when he saw her toy, and gibe, and geare,
And passe the bonds of modest merimake,
Her dalliaunce he despisd, and follies did forsake.

XXII
Yet she still followed her former style,
And said, and did, all that mote him delight,
Till they arrived in that pleasaunt ile,
Where sleeping late she lefte her other knight.
But whenas Guyon of that land had sight,
He wist him selfe amisse, and angry said:
'Ah! dame, perdy ye have not doen me right,
Thus to mislead mee, whiles I you obaid:
Me litle needed from my right way to have straid.'

XXIII
'Faire sir,' quoth she, 'be not displeasd at all:
Who fares on sea may not commaund his way,
Ne wind and weather at his pleasure call:
The sea is wide, and easy for to stray;
The wind unstable, and doth never stay.
But here a while ye may in safety rest,
Till season serve new passage to assay:
Better safe port, then be in seas distrest.'
Therewith she laught, and did her earnest end in jest.

XXIV
But he, halfe discontent, mote nathelesse
Himselfe appease, and issewd forth on shore:
The joyes whereof, and happy fruitfulnesse,
Such as he saw, she gan him lay before,
And all, though pleasaunt, yet she made much more:
The fields did laugh, the flowres did freshly spring,
The trees did bud, and early blossomes bore,
And all the quire of birds did sweetly sing,
And told that gardins pleasures in their caroling.

XXV
And she, more sweete then any bird on bough,
Would oftentimes emongst them beare a part,
And strive to passe (as she could well enough)
Their native musicke by her skilful art:
So did she all, that might his constant hart
Withdraw from thought of warlike enterprize,
And drowne in dissolute delights apart,
Where noise of armes, or vew of martiall guize,
Might not revive desire of knightly exercize.

XXVI
But he was wise, and wary of her will,
And ever held his hand upon his hart:
Yet would not seeme so rude, and thewed ill,
As to despise so curteous seeming part,
That gentle lady did to him impart:
But fairly tempring fond desire subdewd,
And ever her desired to depart.
She list not heare, but her disports poursewd,
And ever bad him stay, till time the tide renewd.

XXVII
And now by this, Cymochles howre was spent,
That he awoke out of his ydle dreme,
And shaking off his drowsy dreriment,
Gan him avize, howe ill did him beseme,
In slouthfull sleepe his molten hart to steme,
And quench the brond of his conceived yre.
Tho up he started, stird with shame extreme,
Ne staied for his damsell to inquire,
But marched to the strond, there passage to require.

XXVIII
And in the way he with Sir Guyon mett,
Accompanyde with Phædria the faire:
Eftsoones he gan to rage, and inly frett,
Crying: 'Let be that lady debonaire,
Thou recreaunt knight, and soone thy selfe prepaire
To batteile, if thou meane her love to gayn:
Loe! loe already, how the fowles in aire
Doe flocke, awaiting shortly to obtayn
Thy carcas for their pray, the guerdon of thy payn.'

XXIX
And therewithall he fiersly at him flew,
And with importune outrage him assayld;
Who, soone prepard to field, his sword forth drew,
And him with equall valew countervayld:
Their mightie strokes their haberjeons dismayld,
And naked made each others manly spalles;
The mortall steele despiteously entayld
Deepe in their flesh, quite through the yron walles,
That a large purple stream adown their giambeux falles.

XXX
Cymocles, that had never mett before
So puissant foe, with envious despight
His prowd presumed force increased more,
Disdeigning to bee held so long in fight:
Sir Guyon, grudging not so much his might,
As those unknightly raylinges which he spoke,

With wrathfull fire his corage kindled bright,
Thereof devising shortly to be wroke,
And, doubling all his powres, redoubled every stroke.

XXXI
Both of them high attonce their hands enhaunst,
And both attonce their huge blowes down did sway:
Cymochles sword on Guyons shield ygalunst,
And thereof nigh one quarter sheard away;
But Guyons angry blade so fiers did play
On th' others helmett, which as Titan shone,
That quite it clove his plumed crest in tway,
And bared all his head unto the bone;
Wherewith astonisht, still he stood, as sencelesse stone.

XXXII
Still as he stood, fayre Phædria, that beheld
That deadly daunger, soone atweene them ran;
And at their feet her selfe most humbly feld,
Crying with pitteous voyce, and count'nance wan,
'Ah, well away! most noble lords, how can
Your cruell eyes endure so pitteous sight,
To shed your lives on ground? Wo worth the man,
That first did teach the cursed steele to bight
In his owne flesh, and make way to the living spright!

XXXIII
'If ever love of lady did empierce
Your yron brestes, or pittie could find place,
Withhold your bloody handes from battaill fierce,
And sith for me ye fight, to me this grace
Both yield, to stay your deadly stryfe a space.'
They stayd a while; and forth she gan proceed:
'Most wretched woman, and of wicked race,
That am the authour of this hainous deed,
And cause of death betweene two doughtie knights do breed!

XXXIV
'But if for me ye fight, or me will serve,
Not this rude kynd of battaill, nor these armes
Are meet, the which doe men in bale to sterve,
And doolefull sorrow heape with deadly harmes:
Such cruell game my scarmoges disarmes:
Another warre, and other weapons, I
Doe love, where Love does give his sweet alarmes,
Without bloodshed, and where the enimy
Does yield unto his foe a pleasaunt victory.

XXXV
'Debatefull strife, and cruell enmity,
The famous name of knighthood fowly shend;

But lovely peace, and gentle amity,
And in amours the passing howres to spend,
The mightie martiall handes doe most commend;
Of love they ever greater glory bore,
Then of their armes: Mars is Cupidoes frend,
And is for Venus loves renowmed more,
Then all his wars and spoiles, the which he did of yore.'

XXXVI

Therewith she sweetly smyld. They, though full bent
To prove extremities of bloody fight,
Yet at her speach their rages gan relent,
And calme the sea of their tempestuous spight:
Such powre have pleasing wordes; such is the might
Of courteous clemency in gentle hart.
Now after all was ceast, the Faery knight
Besought that damzell suffer him depart,
And yield him ready passage to that other part.

XXXVII

She no lesse glad, then he desirous, was
Of his departure thence; for of her joy
And vaine delight she saw he light did pas,
A foe of folly and immodest toy,
Still solemne sad, or still disdainfull coy,
Delighting all in armes and cruell warre,
That her sweet peace and pleasures did annoy,
Troubled with terrour and unquiet jarre,
That she well pleased was thence to amove him farre.

XXXVIII

Tho him she brought abord, and her swift bote
Forthwith directed to that further strand;
The which on the dull waves did lightly flote,
And soone arrived on the shallow sand,
Where gladsome Guyon salied forth to land,
And to that damsell thankes gave for reward.
Upon that shore he spyed Atin stand,
There by his maister left when late he far'd
In Phædrias flitt barck over that perlous shard.

XXXIX

Well could he him remember, sith of late
He with Pyrochles sharp debatement made:
Streight gan he him revyle, and bitter rate,
As shepheardes curre, that in darke eveninges shade
Hath tracted forth some salvage beastes trade:
'Vile miscreaunt!' said he, 'whether dost thou flye
The shame and death, which will thee soone invade?
What coward hand shall doe thee next to dye,
That art thus fowly fledd from famous enimy?'

XL
With that he stifly shooke his steelhead dart:
But sober Guyon hearin him so rayle,
Though somewhat moved in his mightie hart,
Yet with strong reason maistred passion fraile,
And passed fayrely forth. He, turning taile,
Backe to the strond retyrd, and there still stayd,
A waiting passage, which him late did faile;
The whiles Cymochles with that wanton mayd
The hasty heat of his avowd revenge delayd.

XLI
Whylest there the varlet stood, he saw from farre
An armed knight, that towardes him fast ran;
He ran on foot, as if in lucklesse warre
His forlorne steed from him the victour wan;
He seemed breathlesse, hartlesse, faint, and wan,
And all his armour sprinckled was with blood,
And soyld with durtie gore, that no man can
Discerne the hew thereof. He never stood,
But bent his hastie course towardes the ydle flood.

XLII
The varlett saw, when to the flood he came,
How without stop or stay he fiersly lept,
And deepe him selfe beducked in the same,
That in the lake his loftie crest was stept,
Ne of his safetie seemed care he kept,
But with his raging armes he rudely flasht
The waves about, and all his armour swept,
That all the blood and filth away was washt,
Yet still he bet the water, and the billowes dasht.

XLIII
Atin drew nigh, to weet what it mote bee;
For much he wondred at that uncouth sight:
Whom should he, but his own deare lord, there see,
His owne deare lord Pyrochles in sad plight,
Ready to drowne him selfe for fell despight.
'Harrow now out, and well away!' he cryde,
'What dismall day hath lent this cursed light,
To see my lord so deadly damnifyde?
Pyrochles, O Pyrochles, what is thee betyde?'

XLIV
'I burne, I burne, I burne!' then lowd he cryde,
'O how I burne with implacable fyre!
Yet nought can quench mine inly flaming syde,
Nor sea of licour cold, nor lake of myre,
Nothing but death can doe me to respyre.'

'Ah! be it,' said he, 'from Pyrochles farre,
After pursewing Death once to requyre,
Or think, that ought those puissant hands may marre:
Death is for wretches borne under unhappy starre.'

XLV
'Perdye, then is it fitt for me,' said he,
'That am, I weene, most wretched man alive,
Burning in flames, yet no flames can I see,
And dying dayly, dayly yet revive.
O Atin, helpe to me last death to give.'
The varlet at his plaint was grieved so sore,
That his deepe wounded hart in two did rive,
And his owne health remembring now no more,
Did follow that ensample which he blam'd afore.

XLVI
Into the lake he lept, his lord to ayd,
(So love the dread of daunger doth despise)
And of him catching hold, him strongly stayd
From drowning. But more happy he then wise,
Of that seas nature did him not avise.
The waves thereof so slow and sluggish were,
Engrost with mud, which did them fowle agrise,
That every weighty thing they did upbeare,
Ne ought mote ever sinck downe to the bottom there.

XLVII
Whiles thus they strugled in that ydle wave,
And strove in vaine, the one him selfe to drowne,
The other both from drowning for to save,
Lo! to that shore one in an aunciount gowne,
Whose hoary locks great gravitie did crowne,
Holding in hand a goodly arming sword,
By fortune came, ledd with the troublous sowne:
Where drenched deepe he fownd in that dull ford
The carefull servaunt, stryving with his raging lord.

XLVIII
Him Atin spying, knew right well of yore,
And lowdly cald: 'Help, helpe! O Archimage,
To save my lord, in wretched plight forlore;
Helpe with thy hand, or with thy counsell sage:
Weake handes, but counsell is most strong in age.'
Him when the old man saw, he woundred sore,
To see Pyrochles there so rudely rage:
Yet sithens helpe, he saw, he needed more
Then pitty, he in hast approched to the shore;

XLIX
And cald, 'Pyrochles! what is this I see?

What hellish fury hath at earst thee hent?
Furious ever I thee knew to bee,
Yet never in this straunge astonishment.'
'These flames, these flames,' he cryde, 'do me torment!'
'What flames,' quoth he, 'when I thee present see
In daunger rather to be drent then brent?'
'Harrow! the flames which me consume,' said hee,
'Ne can be quencht, within my secret bowelles bee.

L
'That cursed man, that cruel feend of hell,
Furor, oh! Furor hath me thus bedight:
His deadly woundes within my liver swell,
And his whott fyre burnes in mine entralles bright,
Kindled through his infernall brond of spight,
Sith late with him I batteill vaine would boste;
That now I weene Joves dreaded thunder light
Does scorch not halfe so sore, nor damned ghoste
In flaming Phlegeton does not so felly roste.'

LI
Which when as Archimago heard, his griefe
He knew right well, and him attonce disarmd:
Then searcht his secret woundes, and made a priefe
Of every place, that was with bruzing harmd,
Or with the hidden fire too inly warmd.
Which doen, he balmes and herbes thereto applyde,
And evermore with mightie spels them charmd,
That in short space he has them qualifyde,
And him restor'd to helth, that would have algates dyde.

CANTO VII

Guyon findes Mamon in a delve,
Sunning his threasure hore:
Is by him tempted, and led downe,
To see his secrete store.

I
As pilot well expert in perilous wave,
That to a stedfast starre his course hath bent,
When foggy mistes or cloudy tempests have
The faith full light of that faire lampe yblent,
And cover'd heaven with hideous dreriment,
Upon his card and compas firmes his eye,
The maysters of his long experiment,
And to them does the steddy helme apply,

Bidding his winged vessell fairely forward fly:

II
So Guyon, having lost his trustie guyde,
Late left beyond that Ydle Lake, proceedes
Yet on his way, of none accompanyde;
And evermore himselfe with comfort feedes
Of his owne vertues and praise-worthie deedes.
So long he yode, yet no adventure found,
Which Fame of her shrill trompet worthy reedes:
For still he traveild through wide wastfull ground,
That nought but desert wildernesse shewed all around.

III
At last he came unto a gloomy glade,
Cover'd with boughes and shrubs from heavens light,
Whereas he sitting found in secret shade
An uncouth, salvage, and uncivile wight,
Of griesly hew and fowle ill favour'd sight;
His face with smoke was tand, and eies were bleard,
His head and beard with sout were ill bedight,
His cole-blacke hands did seeme to have ben seard
In smythes fire-spitting forge, and nayles like clawes appeard.

IV
His yron cote, all overgrowne with rust,
Was underneath enveloped with gold,
Whose glistring glosse, darkned with filthy dust,
Well yet appeared to have beene of old
A worke of rich entayle and curious mould,
Woven with antickes and wyld ymagery:
And in his lap a masse of coyne he told,
And turned upside downe, to feede his eye
And covetous desire with his huge threasury.

V
And round about him lay on every side
Great heapes of gold, that never could be spent:
Of which some were rude owre, not purifide
Of Mulcibers devouring element;
Some others were new driven, and distent
Into great ingowes, and to wedges square;
Some in round plates withouten moniment:
But most were stampt, and in their metal bare
The antique shapes of kings and kesars straung and rare.

VI
Soone as he Guyon saw, in great affright
And haste he rose, for to remove aside
Those pretious hils from straungers envious sight,
And downe them poured through an hole full wide

Into the hollow earth, them there to hide.
But Guyon, lightly to him leaping, stayd
His hand, that trembled as one terrifyde;
And though him selfe were at the sight dismayd,
Yet him perforce restraynd, and to him doubtfull sayd:

VII
'What art thou, man, (if man at all thou art)
That here in desert hast thine habitaunce,
And these rich heapes of welth doest hide apart
From the worldes eye, and from her right usaunce?'
Thereat, with staring eyes fixed askaunce,
In great disdaine, he answerd: 'Hardy Elfe,
That darest vew my direfull countenaunce,
I read thee rash and heedlesse of thy selfe,
To trouble my still seate, and heapes of pretious pelfe.

VIII
'God of the world and worldlings I me call,
Great Mammon, greatest god below the skye,
That of my plenty poure out unto all,
And unto none my graces do envye:
Riches, renowme, and principality,
Honour, estate, and all this worldes good,
For which men swinck and sweat incessantly,
Fro me do flow into an ample flood,
And in the hollow earth have their eternall brood.

IX
'Wherefore, if me thou deigne to serve and sew,
At thy commaund, lo! all these mountaines bee;
Or if to thy great mind, or greedy vew,
All these may not suffise, there shall to thee
Ten times so much be nombred francke and free.'
'Mammon,' said he, 'thy godheads vaunt is vaine,
And idle offers of thy golden fee;
To them that covet such eye-glutting gaine
Proffer thy giftes, and fitter servaunts entertaine.

X
'Me ill besits, that in derdoing armes
And honours suit my vowed daies do spend,
Unto thy bounteous baytes and pleasing charmes,
With which weake men thou witchest, to attend:
Regard of worldly mucke doth fowly blend
And low abase the high heroicke spright,
That joyes for crownes and kingdomes to contend;
Faire shields, gay steedes, bright armes be my delight:
Those be the riches fit for an advent'rous knight.'

XI

'Vaine glorious Elfe,' saide he, 'doest not thou weet,
That money can thy wantes at will supply?
Sheilds, steeds, and armes, and all things for thee meet
It can purvay in twinckling of an eye;
And crownes and kingdomes to thee multiply.
Doe not I kings create, and throw the crowne
Sometimes to him that low in dust doth ly?
And him that raignd into his rowme thrust downe,
And whom I lust do heape with glory and renowne?'

XII
'All otherwise, saide he, 'I riches read,
And deeme them roote of all disquietnesse;
First got with guile, and then preserv'd with dread,
And after spent with pride and lavishnesse,
Leaving behind them griefe and heavinesse.
Infinite mischiefes of them doe arize,
Strife and debate, bloodshed and bitternesse,
Outrageous wrong and hellish covetize,
That noble heart, as great dishonour, doth despize.

XIII
'Ne thine be kingdomes, ne the scepters thine;
But realmes and rulers thou doest both confound,
And loyall truth to treason doest incline:
Witnesse the guiltlesse blood pourd oft on ground,
The crowned often slaine, the slayer cround,
The sacred diademe in peeces rent,
And purple robe gored with many a wound;
Castles surprizd, great citties sackt and brent:
So mak'st thou kings, and gaynest wrongfull government.

XIV
'Long were to tell the troublous stormes, that thosse
The private state, and make the life unsweet:
Who swelling sayles in Caspian sea doth crosse,
And in frayle wood on Adrian gulf doth fleet,
Doth not, I weene, so many evils meet.'
Then Mammon, wexing wroth, 'And why then,' sayd,
'Are mortall men so fond and undiscreet,
So evill thing to seeke unto their ayd,
And having not, complaine, and having it, upbrayd?'

XV
'Indeede,' quoth he, 'through fowle intemperaunce,
Frayle men are oft captiv'd to covetise:
But would they thinke, with how small allowaunce
Untroubled nature doth her selfe suffise,
Such superfluities they would despise,
Which with sad cares empeach our native joyes:
At the well head the purest streames arise:

But mucky filth his braunching armes annoyes,
And with uncomely weedes the gentle wave accloyes.

XVI
'The antique world, in his first flowring youth,
Fownd no defect in his Creators grace,
But with glad thankes, and unreproved truth,
The guifts of soveraine bounty did embrace:
Like angels life was then mens happy cace:
But later ages pride, like corn-fed steed,
Abusd her plenty and fat swolne encreace
To all licentious lust, and gan exceed
The measure of her meane, and naturall first need.

XVII
'Then gan a cursed hand the quiet wombe
Of his great grandmother with steele to wound,
And the hid treasures in her sacred tombe
With sacriledge to dig. Therein he fownd
Fountaines of gold and silver to abownd,
Of which the matter of his huge desire
And pompous pride eftsoones he did compownd;
Then avarice gan through his veines inspire
His greedy flames, and kindled life-devouring fire.'

XVIII
'Sonne,' said he then, 'lett be thy bitter scorne,
And leave the rudenesse of that antique age
To them that liv'd therin in state forlorne.
Thou, that doest live in later times, must wage
Thy workes for wealth, and life for gold engage.
If then thee list my offred grace to use,
Take what thou please of all this surplusage;
If thee list not, leave have thou to refuse:
But thing refused doe not afterward accuse.'

XIX
'Me list not,' said the Elfin knight, 'receave
Thing offred, till I know it well be gott;
Ne wote I, but thou didst these goods bereave
From rightfull owner by unrighteous lott,
Or that blood guiltinesse or guile them blott.'
'Perdy,' quoth he, 'yet never eie did vew,
Ne tong did tell, ne hand these handled not;
But safe I have them kept in secret mew
From hevens sight, and powre of al which them poursew.'

XX
'What secret place,' quoth he, 'can safely hold
So huge a masse, and hide from heavens eie?
Or where hast thou thy wonne, that so much gold

Thou canst preserve from wrong and robbery?'
'Come thou,' quoth he, 'and see.' So by and by,
Through that thick covert he him led, and fownd
A darkesome way, which no man could descry,
That deep descended through the hollow grownd,
And was with dread and horror compassed arownd.

XXI
At length they came into a larger space,
That stretcht it selfe into an ample playne,
Through which a beaten broad high way did trace,
That streight did lead to Plutoes griesly rayne:
By that wayes side there sate infernall Payne,
And fast beside him sat tumultuous Strife:
The one in hand an yron whip did strayne,
The other brandished a bloody knife,
And both did gnash their teeth, and both did threten life.

XXII
On thother side, in one consort, there sate
Cruell Revenge, and rancorous Despight,
Disloyall Treason, and hart-burning Hate;
But gnawing Gealosy, out of their sight
Sitting alone, his bitter lips did bight;
And trembling Feare still to and fro did fly,
And found no place, wher safe he shroud him might;
Lamenting Sorrow did in darknes lye;
And Shame his ugly face did hide from living eye.

XXIII
And over them sad Horror with grim hew
Did alwaies sore, beating his yron wings;
And after him owles and night-ravens flew,
The hatefull messengers of heavy things,
Of death and dolor telling sad tidings;
Whiles sad Celeno, sitting on a clifte,
A song of bale and bitter sorrow sings,
That hart of flint a sonder could have rifte:
Which having ended, after him she flyeth swifte.

XXIV
All these before the gates of Pluto lay;
By whom they passing, spake unto them nought.
But th' Elfin knight with wonder all the way
Did feed his eyes, and fild his inner thought,
At last him to a litle dore he brought,
That to the gate of hell, which gaped wide,
Was next adjoyning, ne them parted ought:
Betwixt them both was but a litle stride,
That did the house of Richesse from hell-mouth divide.

XXV
Before the dore sat selfe-consuming Care,
Day and night keeping wary watch and ward,
For feare least Force or Fraud should unaware
Breake in, and spoile the treasure there in gard:
Ne would he suffer Sleepe once thetherward
Approch, albe his drowsy den were next;
For next to Death is Sleepe to be compard:
Therefore his house is unto his annext;
Here Sleep, ther Richesse, and helgate them both betwext.

XXVI
So soone as Mammon there arrivd, the dore
To him did open and affoorded way;
Him followed eke Sir Guyon evermore,
Ne darkenesse him, ne daunger might dismay.
Soone as he entred was, the dore streight way
Did shutt, and from behind it forth there lept
An ugly feend, more fowle then dismall day,
The which with monstrous stalke behind him stept,
And ever as he went, dew watch upon him kept.

XXVII
Well hoped hee, ere long that hardy guest,
If ever covetous hand, or lustfull eye,
Or lips he layd on thing that likte him best,
Or ever sleepe his eiestrings did untye,
Should be his pray. And therefore still on hye
He over him did hold his cruell clawes,
Threatning with greedy gripe to doe him dye,
And rend in peeces with his ravenous pawes,
If ever he transgrest the fatall Stygian lawes.

XXVIII
That houses forme within was rude and strong,
Lyke an huge cave, hewne out of rocky clifte,
From whose rough vaut the ragged breaches hong,
Embost with massy gold of glorious guifte,
And with rich metall loaded every rifte,
That heavy ruine they did seeme to threatt;
And over them Arachne high did lifte
Her cunning web, and spred her subtile nett,
Enwrapped in fowle smoke and clouds more black then jett.

XXIX
Both roofe, and floore, and walls were all of gold,
But overgrowne with dust and old decay,
And hid in darkenes, that none could behold
The hew thereof: for vew of cherefull day
Did never in that house it selfe display,
But a faint shadow of uncertein light;

Such as a lamp, whose life does fade away;
Or as the moone, cloathed with clowdy night,
Does shew to him that walkes in feare and sad affright.

XXX
In all that rowme was nothing to be seene,
But huge great yron chests and coffers strong,
All bard with double bends, that none could weene
Them to efforce by violence or wrong:
On every side they placed were along.
But all the grownd with sculs was scattered,
And dead mens bones, which round about were flong;
Whose lives, it seemed, whilome there were shed,
And their vile carcases now left unburied.

XXXI
They forward passe, ne Guyon yet spoke word,
Till that they came unto an yron dore,
Which to them opened of his owne accord,
And shewd of richesse such exceeding store,
As eie of man did never see before,
Ne ever could within one place be fownd,
Though all the wealth, which is, or was of yore,
Could gathered be through all the world arownd,
And that above were added to that under grownd.

XXXII
The charge thereof unto a covetous spright
Commaunded was, who thereby did attend,
And warily awaited day and night,
From other covetous feends it to defend,
Who it to rob and ransacke did intend.
Then Mammon, turning to that warriour, said:
'Loe here the worldes blis! loe here the end,
To which al men doe ayme, rich to be made!
Such grace now to be happy is before thee laid.'

XXXIII
'Certes,' sayd he, 'I n'ill thine offred grace,
Ne to be made so happy doe intend:
Another blis before mine eyes I place,
Another happines, another end.
To them that list, these base regardes I lend:
But I in armes, and in atchievements brave,
Do rather choose my flitting houres to spend,
And to be lord of those that riches have,
Then them to have my selfe, and be their servile sclave.'

XXXIV
Thereat the feend his gnashing teeth did grate,
And griev'd, so long to lacke his greedie pray;

For well he weened that so glorious bayte
Would tempt his guest to take thereof assay:
Had he so doen, he had him snatcht away,
More light then culver in the faulcons fist.
Eternall God thee save from such decay!
But whenas Mammon saw his purpose mist,
Him to entrap unwares another way he wist.

XXXV
Thence forward he him ledd, and shortly brought
Unto another rowme, whose dore forthright
To him did open, as it had beene taught:
Therein an hundred raunges weren pight,
And hundred fournaces all burning bright:
By every fournace many feendes did byde,
Deformed creatures, horrible in sight;
And every feend his busie paines applyde,
To melt the golden metall, ready to be tryde.

XXXVI
One with great bellowes gathered filling ayre,
And with forst wind the fewell did inflame;
Another did the dying bronds repayre
With yron tongs, and sprinckled ofte the same
With liquid waves, fiers Vulcans rage to tame,
Who, maystring them, renewd his former heat;
Some scumd the drosse, that from the metall came,
Some stird the molten owre with ladles great;
And every one did swincke, and every one did sweat.

XXXVII
But when an earthly wight they present saw,
Glistring in armes and battailous aray,
From their whot work they did themselves withdraw
To wonder at the sight: for, till that day,
They never creature saw, that cam that way.
Their staring eyes, sparckling with fervent fyre,
And ugly shapes did nigh the man dismay,
That, were it not for shame, he would retyre;
Till that him thus bespake their soveraine lord and syre:

XXXVIII
'Behold, thou Faeries sonne, with mortall eye,
That living eye before did never see:
The thing that thou didst crave so earnestly
To weet, whence all the wealth late shewd by mee
Proceeded, lo! now is reveald to thee.
Here is the fountaine of the worldes good:
Now therefore, if thou wilt enriched bee,
Avise thee well, and chaunge thy wilfull mood;
Least thou perhaps hereafter wish, and be withstood.'

XXXIX
'Suffise it then, thou Money God,' quoth hee,
'That all thine ydle offers I refuse.
All that I need I have; what needeth mee
To covet more then I have cause to use?
With such vaine shewes thy worldlinges vyle abuse:
But give me leave to follow mine emprise.'
Mammon was much displeasd, yet no'te he chuse
But beare the rigour of his bold mesprise,
And thence him forward ledd, him further to entise.

XL
He brought him through a darksom narrow strayt,
To a broad gate, all built of beaten gold:
The gate was open, but therein did wayt
A sturdie villein, stryding stiffe and bold,
As if that Highest God defy he would:
In his right hand an yron club he held,
But he himselfe was all of golden mould,
Yet had both life and sence, and well could weld
That cursed weapon, when his cruell foes he queld.

XLI
Disdayne he called was, and did disdayne
To be so cald, and who so did him call:
Sterne was his looke, and full of stomacke vayne,
His portaunce terrible, and stature tall,
Far passing th' hight of men terrestriall,
Like an huge gyant of the Titans race;
That made him scorne all creatures great and small,
And with his pride all others powre deface:
More fitt emongst black fiendes then men to have his place.

XLII
Soone as those glitterand armes he did espye,
That with their brightnesse made that darknes light,
His harmefull club he gan to hurtle hye,
And threaten batteill to the Faery knight;
Who likewise gan himselfe to batteill dight,
Till Mammon did his hasty hand withhold,
And counseld him abstaine from perilous fight:
For nothing might abash the villein bold,
Ne mortall steele emperce his miscreated mould.

XLIII
So having him with reason pacifyde,
And the fiers carle commaunding to forbeare,
He brought him in. The rowme was large and wyde,
As it some gyeld or solemne temple weare:
Many great golden pillours did upbeare

The massy roofe, and riches huge sustayne,
And every pillour decked was full deare
With crownes, and diademes, and titles vaine,
Which mortall princes wore, whiles they on earth did rayne.

XLIV
A route of people there assembled were,
Of every sort and nation under skye,
Which with great uprore preaced to draw nere
To th' upper part, where was advaunced hye
A stately siege of soveraine majestye;
And thereon satt a woman gorgeous gay,
And richly cladd in robes of royaltye,
That never earthly prince in such aray
His glory did enhaunce and pompous pryde display.

XLV
Her face right wondrous faire did seeme to bee,
That her broad beauties beam great brightnes threw
Through the dim shade, that all men might it see:
Yet was not that same her owne native hew,
But wrought by art and counterfetted shew,
Thereby more lovers unto her to call;
Nath'lesse most hevenly faire in deed and vew
She by creation was, till she did fall;
Thenceforth she sought for helps to cloke her crime withall.

XLVI
There as in glistring glory she did sitt,
She held a great gold chaine ylincked well,
Whose upper end to highest heven was knitt,
And lower part did reach to lowest hell;
And all that preace did rownd about her swell,
To catchen hold of that long chaine, thereby
To climbe aloft, and others to excell:
That was Ambition, rash desire to sty,
And every linck thereof a step of dignity.

XLVII
Some thought to raise themselves to high degree
By riches and unrighteous reward;
Some by close shouldring, some by flatteree;
Others through friendes, others for base regard;
And all by wrong waies for themselves prepard.
Those that were up themselves, kept others low,
Those that were low themselves, held others hard,
Ne suffred them to ryse or greater grow,
But every one did strive his fellow downe to throw.

XLVIII
Which whenas Guyon saw, he gan inquire,

What meant that preace about that ladies throne,
And what she was that did so high aspyre.
Him Mammon answered: 'That goodly one,
Whom all that folke with such contention
Doe flock about, my deare, my daughter is:
Honour and dignitie from her alone
Derived are, and all this worldes blis,
For which ye men doe strive: few gett, but many mis.

XLIX
'And fayre Philotime she rightly hight,
The fairest wight that wonneth under skye,
But that this darksom neather world her light
Doth dim with horror and deformity,
Worthie of heven and hye felicitie,
From whence the gods have her for envy thrust:
But sith thou hast found favour in mine eye,
Thy spouse I will her make, if that thou lust,
That she may thee advance for works and merits just.'

L
'Gramercy, Mammon,' said the gentle knight,
'For so great grace and offred high estate,
But I, that am fraile flesh and earthly wight,
Unworthy match for such immortall mate
My selfe well wote, and mine unequall fate:
And were I not, yet is my trouth yplight,
And love avowd to other lady late,
That to remove the same I have no might:
To chaunge love causelesse is reproch to warlike knight.'

LI
Mammon emmoved was with inward wrath;
Yet, forcing it to fayne, him forth thence ledd,
Through griesly shadowes by a beaten path,
Into a gardin goodly garnished
With hearbs and fruits, whose kinds mote not be redd:
Not such as earth out of her fruitfull woomb
Throwes forth to men, sweet and well savored,
But direfull deadly black, both leafe and bloom,
Fitt to adorne the dead and deck the drery toombe.

LII
There mournfull cypresse grew in greatest store,
And trees of bitter gall, and heben sad,
Dead sleeping poppy, and black hellebore,
Cold coloquintida, and tetra mad,
Mortall samnitis, and cicuta bad,
With which th' unjust Atheniens made to dy
Wise Socrates, who thereof quaffing glad,
Pourd out his life and last philosophy

To the fayre Critias, his dearest belamy.

LIII
The Gardin of Proserpina this hight;
And in the midst thereof a silver seat,
With a thick arber goodly overdight,
In which she often usd from open heat
Her selfe to shroud, and pleasures to entreat.
Next thereunto did grow a goodly tree,
With braunches broad dispredd and body great,
Clothed with leaves, that none the wood mote see,
And loaden all with fruit as thick as it might bee.

LIV
Their fruit were golden apples glistring bright,
That goodly was their glory to behold;
On earth like never grew, ne living wight
Like ever saw, but they from hence were sold;
For those, which Hercules with conquest bold
Got from great Atlas daughters, hence began,
And, planted there, did bring forth fruit of gold;
And those with which th' Eubœan young man wan
Swift Atalanta, when through craft he her out ran.

LV
Here also sprong that goodly golden fruit,
With which Acontius got his lover trew,
Whom he had long time sought with fruitlesse suit:
Here eke that famous golden apple grew,
The which emongst the gods false Ate threw;
For which th' Idæan ladies disagreed,
Till partiall Paris dempt it Venus dew,
And had of her fayre Helen for his meed,
That many noble Greekes and Trojans made to bleed.

LVI
The warlike Elfe much wondred at this tree,
So fayre and great, that shadowed all the ground,
And his broad braunches, laden with rich fee,
Did stretch themselves without the utmost bound
Of this great gardin, compast with a mound:
Which over-hanging, they themselves did steepe
In a blacke flood, which flow'd about it round;
That is the river of Cocytus deepe,
In which full many soules do endlesse wayle and weepe.

LVII
Which to behold, he clomb up to the bancke,
And, looking downe, saw many damned wightes,
In those sad waves, which direfull deadly stancke,
Plonged continually of cruell sprightes,

That with their piteous cryes, and yelling shrightes,
They made the further shore resounden wide.
Emongst the rest of those same ruefull sightes,
One cursed creature he by chaunce espide,
That drenched lay full deepe, under the garden side.

LVIII
Deepe was he drenched to the upmost chin,
Yet gaped still, as coveting to drinke
Of the cold liquour which he waded in,
And stretching forth his hand, did often thinke
To reach the fruit which grew upon the brincke:
But both the fruit from hand, and flood from mouth,
Did fly abacke, and made him vainely swincke:
The whiles he serv'd with hunger and with drouth,
He daily dyde, yet never throughly dyen couth.

LIX
The knight, him seeing labour so in vaine,
Askt who he was, and what he ment thereby:
Who, groning deepe, thus answerd him againe:
'Most cursed of all creatures under skye,
Lo! Tantalus, I here tormented lye:
Of whom high Jove wont whylome feasted bee,
Lo! here I now for want of food doe dye:
But if that thou be such as I thee see,
Of grace I pray thee, give to eat and drinke to mee.'

LX
'Nay, nay, thou greedy Tantalus,' quoth he,
'Abide the fortune of thy present fate,
And unto all that live in high degree
Ensample be of mind intemperate,
To teach them how to use their present state.'
Then gan the cursed wretch alowd to cry,
Accusing highest Jove and gods ingrate,
And eke blaspheming heaven bitterly,
As authour of unjustice, there to let him dye.

LXI
He lookt a litle further, and espyde
Another wretch, whose carcas deepe was drent
Within the river, which the same did hyde:
But both his handes, most filthy feculent,
Above the water were on high extent,
And faynd to wash themselves incessantly;
Yet nothing cleaner were for such intent,
But rather fowler seemed to the eye;
So lost his labour vaine and ydle industry.

LXII

The knight, him calling, asked who he was;
Who, lifting up his head, him answerd thus:
'I Pilate am, the falsest judge, alas!
And most unjust; that, by unrighteous
And wicked doome, to Jewes despiteous
Delivered up the Lord of Life to dye,
And did acquite a murdrer felonous:
The whiles my handes I washt in purity,
The whiles my soule was soyld with fowle iniquity.'

LXIII
Infinite moe, tormented in like paine,
He there beheld, too long here to be told:
Ne Mammon would there let him long remayne,
For terrour of the tortures manifold,
In which the damned soules he did behold,
But roughly him bespake: 'Thou fearefull foole,
Why takest not of that same fruite of gold,
Ne sittest downe on that same silver stoole,
To rest thy weary person in the shadow coole?'

LXIV
All which he did, to do him deadly fall
In frayle intemperaunce through sinfull bayt;
To which if he inclyned had at all,
That dreadfull feend, which did behinde him wayt,
Would him have rent in thousand peeces strayt:
But he was wary wise in all his way,
And well perceived his deceiptfull sleight,
Ne suffred lust his safety to betray;
So goodly did beguile the guyler of his pray.

LXV
And now he has so long remained theare,
That vitall powres gan wexe both weake and wan,
For want of food and sleepe, which two upbeare,
Like mightie pillours, this frayle life of man,
That none without the same enduren can.
For now three dayes of men were full outwrought,
Since he this hardy enterprize began:
Forthy great Mammon fayrely he besought,
Into the world to guyde him backe, as he him brought.

LXVI
The god, though loth, yet was constraynd t' obay,
For, lenger time then that, no living wight
Below the earth might suffred be to stay:
So backe againe him brought to living light.
But all so soone as his enfeebled spright
Gan sucke this vitall ayre into his brest,
As overcome with too exceeding might,

The life did flit away out of her nest,
And all his sences were with deadly fit opprest.

CANTO VIII

Sir Guyon, layd in swowne, is by
Acrates sonnes despoyld;
Whom Arthure soone hath reskewed
And Paynim brethren foyld.

I
And is there care in heaven? And is there love
In heavenly spirits to these creatures bace,
That may compassion of their evilles move?
There is: else much more wretched were the cace
Of men then beasts. But O th' exceeding grace
Of Highest God, that loves his creatures so,
And all his workes with mercy doth embrace,
That blessed angels he sends to and fro,
To serve to wicked man, to serve his wicked foe!

II
How oft do they their silver bowers leave
To come to succour us, that succour want!
How oft do they with golden pineons cleave
The flitting skyes, like flying pursuivant,
Against fowle feendes to ayd us militant!
They for us fight, they watch and dewly ward,
And their bright squadrons round about us plant;
And all for love, and nothing for reward:
O why should hevenly God to men have such regard?

III
During the while that Guyon did abide
In Mamons house, the palmer, whom whyleare
That wanton mayd of passage had denide,
By further search had passage found elsewhere,
And, being on his way, approched neare
Where Guyon lay in traunce, when suddeinly
He heard a voyce, that called lowd and cleare,
'Come hether! come hether! O come hastily!'
That all the fields resounded with the ruefull cry.

IV
The palmer lent his eare unto the noyce,
To weet who called so importunely:
Againe he heard a more efforced voyce,

That bad him come in haste. He by and by
His feeble feet directed to the cry;
Which to that shady delve him brought at last,
Where Mammon earst did sunne his threasury:
There the good Guyon he found slumbring fast
In senceles dreame; which sight at first him sore aghast.

V
Beside his head there satt a faire young man,
Of wondrous beauty and of freshest yeares,
Whose tender bud to blossome new began,
And florish faire above his equall peares:
His snowy front, curled with golden heares,
Like Phoebus face adornd with sunny rayes,
Divinely shone, and two sharpe winged sheares,
Decked with diverse plumes, like painted jayes,
Were fixed at his backe, to cut his ayery wayes.

VI
Like as Cupido on Idæan hill,
When having laid his cruell bow away,
And mortall arrowes, wherewith he doth fill
The world with murdrous spoiles and bloody pray,
With his faire mother he him dights to play,
And with his goodly sisters, Graces three;
The goddesse, pleased with his wanton play,
Suffers her selfe through sleepe beguild to bee,
The whiles the other ladies mind theyr mery glee.

VII
Whom when the palmer saw, abasht he was
Through fear and wonder, that he nought could say,
Till him the childe bespoke: 'Long lackt, alas!
Hath bene thy faithfull aide in hard assay,
Whiles deadly fitt thy pupill doth dismay.
Behold this heavy sight, thou reverend sire:
But dread of death and dolor doe away;
For life ere long shall to her home retire,
And he, that breathlesse seems, shal corage bold respire.

VIII
'The charge, which God doth unto me arrett,
Of his deare safety, I to thee commend;
Yet will I not forgoe, ne yet forgett,
The care thereof my selfe unto the end,
But evermore him succour, and defend
Against his foe and mine: watch thou, I pray;
For evill is at hand him to offend.'
So having said, eftsoones he gan display
His painted nimble wings, and vanisht quite away.

IX
The palmer seeing his lefte empty place,
And his slow eies beguiled of their sight,
Woxe sore affraid, and standing still a space,
Gaz'd after him, as fowle escapt by flight:
At last him turning to his charge behight,
With trembling hand his troubled pulse gan try,
Where finding life not yet dislodged quight,
He much rejoyst, and courd it tenderly,
As chicken newly hatcht, from dreaded destiny.

X
At last he spide where towards him did pace
Two Paynim knights, al armd as bright as skie,
And them beside an aged sire did trace,
And far before a light-foote page did flie,
That breathed strife and troublous enmitie.
Those were the two sonnes of Acrates old,
Who, meeting earst with Archimago slie,
Foreby that idle strond, of him were told,
That he which earst them combatted was Guyon bold.

XI
Which to avenge on him they dearly vowd,
Where ever that on ground they mote him find:
False Archimage provokte their corage prowd,
And stryful Atin in their stubborne mind
Coles of contention and whot vengeaunce tind.
Now bene they come whereas the Palmer sate,
Keeping that slombred corse to him assind:
Well knew they both his person, sith of late
With him in bloody armes they rashly did debate.

XII
Whom when Pyrochles saw, inflam'd with rage
That sire he fowl bespake: 'Thou dotard vile,
That with thy brutenesse shendst thy comely age,
Abandon soone, I read, the caytive spoile
Of that same outcast carcas, that ere while
Made it selfe famous through false trechery,
And crownd his coward crest with knightly stile:
Loe where he now inglorious doth lye,
To proove he lived il, that did thus fowly dye.'

XIII
To whom the palmer fearlesse answered:
'Certes, sir knight, ye bene too much to blame,
Thus for to blott the honor of the dead,
And with fowle cowardize his carcas shame,
Whose living handes immortalizd his name.
Vile is the vengeaunce on the ashes cold,

And envy base, to barke at sleeping fame:
Was never wight that treason of him told:
Your self his prowesse prov'd, and found him fiers and bold.'

XIV
Then sayd Cymochles: 'Palmer, thou doest dote,
Ne canst of prowesse ne of knighthood deeme,
Save as thou seest or hearst: but well I wote,
That of his puissaunce tryall made extreeme:
Yet gold is not, that doth golden seeme,
Ne all good knights, that shake well speare and shield:
The worth of all men by their end esteeme,
And then dew praise or dew reproch them yield:
Bad therefore I him deeme that thus lies dead on field.'

XV
'Good or bad,' gan his brother fiers reply,
'What doe I recke, sith that he dide entire?
Or what doth his bad death now satisfy
The greedy hunger of revenging yre,
Sith wrathfull hand wrought not her owne desire?
Yet since no way is lefte to wreake my spight,
I will him reave of armes, the victors hire,
And of that shield, more worthy of good knight,
For why should a dead dog be deckt in armour bright?'

XVI
'Fayr sir,' said then the palmer suppliaunt,
'For knighthoods love, doe not so fowle a deed,
Ne blame your honor with so shamefull vaunt
Of vile revenge. To spoile the dead of weed
Is sacrilege, and doth all sinnes exceed;
But leave these relicks of his living might
To decke his herce, and trap his tomb-blacke steed.'
'What herce or steed,' said he, 'should he have dight,
But be entombed in the raven or the kight?'

XVII
With that, rude hand upon his shield he laid,
And th' other brother gan his helme unlace,
Both fiercely bent to have him disaraid;
Till that they spyde where towards them did pace
An armed knight, of bold and bounteous grace,
Whose squire bore after him an heben launce
And coverd shield. Well kend him so far space
Th' enchaunter by his armes and amenaunce,
When under him he saw his Lybian steed to praunce;

XVIII
And to those brethren sayd: 'Rise, rise bylive,
And unto batteil doe your selves addresse;

For yonder comes the prowest knight alive,
Prince Arthur, flowre of grace and nobilesse,
That hath to Paynim knights wrought gret distresse,
And thousand Sar'zins fowly donne to dye.'
That word so deepe did in their harts impresse,
That both eftsoones upstarted furiously,
And gan themselves prepare to batteill greedily.

XIX
But fiers Pyrochles, lacking his owne sword,
The want thereof now greatly gan to plaine,
And Archimage besought, him that afford,
Which he had brought for Braggadochio vaine.
'So would I,' said th' enchaunter, 'glad and faine
Beteeme to you this sword, you to defend,
Or ought that els your honor might maintaine,
But that this weapons powre I well have kend
To be contrary to the worke which ye intend.

XX
'For that same knights owne sword this is, of yore
Which Merlin made by his almightie art
For that his noursling, when he knighthood swore,
Therewith to doen his foes eternall smart.
The metall first he mixt with medæwart,
That no enchauntment from his dint might save;
Then it in flames of Aetna wrought apart,
And seven times dipped in the bitter wave
Of hellish Styx, which hidden vertue to it gave.

XXI
'The vertue is, that nether steele nor stone
The stroke thereof from entraunce may defend;
Ne ever may be used by his fone,
Ne forst his rightful owner to offend;
Ne ever will it breake, ne ever bend:
Wherefore Morddure it rightfully is hight.
In vaine therefore, Pyrochles, should I lend
The same to thee, against his lord to fight,
For sure yt would deceive thy labor and thy might.'

XXII
'Foolish old man,' said then the Pagan wroth,
'That weenest words or charms may force withstond:
Soone shalt thou see, and then beleeve for troth,
That I can carve with this inchaunted brond
His lords owne flesh.' Therewith out of his hond
That vertuous steele he rudely snatcht away,
And Guyons shield about his wrest he bond;
So ready dight, fierce battaile to assay,
And match his brother proud in battailous aray.

XXIII
By this, that straunger knight in presence came,
And goodly salued them; who nought againe
Him answered, as courtesie became,
But with sterne lookes, and stomachous disdaine,
Gave signes of grudge and discontentment vaine:
Then, turning to the palmer, he gan spy
Where at his feet, with sorrowfull demayne
And deadly hew, an armed corse did lye,
In whose dead face he redd great magnanimity.

XXIV
Sayd he then to the palmer: 'Reverend syre,
What great misfortune hath betidd this knight?
Or did his life her fatall date expyre,
Or did he fall by treason, or by fight?
How ever, sure I rew his pitteous plight.'
'Not one, nor other,' sayd the palmer grave,
'Hath him befalne; but cloudes of deadly night
A while his heavy eylids cover'd have,
And all his sences drowned in deep sencelesse wave.

XXV
'Which those his cruell foes, that stand hereby,
Making advauntage, to revenge their spight,
Would him disarme and treaten shamefully;
Unworthie usage of redoubted knight.
But you, faire sir, whose honourable sight
Doth promise hope of helpe and timely grace,
Mote I beseech to succour his sad plight,
And by your powre protect his feeble cace.
First prayse of knighthood is, fowle outrage to deface.'

XXVI
'Palmer,' said he, 'no knight so rude, I weene,
As to doen outrage to a sleeping ghost:
Ne was there ever noble corage seene,
That in advauntage would his puissaunce bost:
Honour is least, where oddes appeareth most.
May bee, that better reason will aswage
The rash revengers heat. Words well dispost
Have secrete powre t' appease inflamed rage:
If not, leave unto me thy knights last patronage.'

XXVII
Tho, turning to those brethren, thus bespoke:
'Ye warlike payre, whose valorous great might,
It seemes, just wronges to vengeaunce doe provoke,
To wreake your wrath on this dead seeming knight,
Mote ought allay the storme of your despight,

And settle patience in so furious heat?
Not to debate the chalenge of your right,
But for this carkas pardon I entreat,
Whom fortune hath already laid in lowest seat.'

XXVIII
To whom Cymochles said: 'For what art thou,
That mak'st thy selfe his dayes-man, to prolong
The vengeaunce prest? Or who shall let me now,
On this vile body from to wreak my wrong,
And make his carkas as the outcast dong?
Why should not that dead carrion satisfye
The guilt which, if he lived had thus long,
His life for dew revenge should deare abye?
The trespas still doth live, albee the person dye.'

XXIX
'Indeed,' then said the Prince, 'the evill donne
Dyes not, when breath the body first doth leave,
But from the grandsyre to the nephewes sonne,
And all his seede, the curse doth often cleave,
Till vengeaunce utterly the guilt bereave:
So streightly God doth judge. But gentle knight,
That doth against the dead his hand upheave,
His honour staines with rancour and despight,
And great disparagment makes to his former might.'

XXX
Pyrochles gan reply the second tyme,
And to him said: 'Now, felon, sure I read,
How that thou art partaker of his cryme:
Therefore by Termagaunt thou shalt be dead.'
With that, his hand, more sad then lomp of lead,
Uplifting high, he weened with Morddure,
His owne good sword Morddure, to cleave his head.
The faithfull steele such treason no'uld endure,
But swarving from the marke, his lordes life did assure.

XXXI
Yet was the force so furious and so fell,
That horse and man it made to reele asyde:
Nath'lesse the Prince would not forsake his sell,
For well of yore he learned had to ryde,
But full of anger fiersly to him cryde:
'False traitour miscreaunt! thou broken hast
The law of armes, to strike foe undefide.
But thou thy treasons fruit, I hope, shalt taste
Right sowre, and feele the law, the which thou hast defast.'

XXXII
With that, his balefull speare he fiercely bent

Against the Pagans brest, and therewith thought
His cursed life out of her lodg have rent:
But ere the point arrivd where it ought,
That seven fold shield, which he from Guyon brought,
He cast between to ward the bitter stownd:
Through all those foldes the steelehead passage wrought,
And through his shoulder perst; wherwith to ground
He groveling fell, all gored in his gushing wound.

XXXIII
Which when his brother saw, fraught with great griefe
And wrath, he to him leaped furiously,
And fowly saide. 'By Mahoune, cursed thiefe,
That direfull stroke thou dearely shalt aby.'
Then, hurling up his harmefull blade on hy,
Smote him so hugely on his haughtie crest,
That from his saddle forced him to fly:
Els mote it needes downe to his manly brest
Have cleft his head in twaine, and life thence dispossest.

XXXIV
Now was the Prince in daungerous distresse,
Wanting his sword, when he on foot should fight:
His single speare could doe him small redresse
Against two foes of so exceeding might,
The least of which was match for any knight.
And now the other, whom he earst did daunt,
Had reard him selfe againe to cruel fight,
Three times more furious and more puissaunt,
Unmindfull of his wound, of his fate ignoraunt.

XXXV
So both attonce him charge on either syde,
With hideous strokes and importable powre,
That forced him his ground to traverse wyde,
And wisely watch to ward that deadly stowre:
For in his shield, as thicke as stormie showre,
Their strokes did raine; yet did he never quaile,
Ne backward shrinke, but as a stedfast towre,
Whom foe with double battry doth assaile,
Them on her bulwarke beares, and bids them nought availe,—

XXXVI
So stoutly he withstood their strong assay;
Till that at last, when he advantage spyde,
His poynant speare he thrust with puissant sway
At proud Cymochles, whiles his shield was wyde,
That through his thigh the mortall steele did gryde:
He, swarving with the force, within his flesh
Did breake the launce, and let the head abyde:
Out of the wound the red blood flowed fresh,

That underneath his feet soone made a purple plesh.

XXXVII
Horribly then he gan to rage and rayle,
Cursing his gods, and him selfe damning deepe:
Als when his brother saw the red blood rayle
Adowne so fast, and all his armour steepe,
For very felnesse lowd he gan to weepe,
And said: 'Caytive, cursse on thy cruell hond,
That twise hath spedd! yet shall it not thee keepe
From the third brunt of this my fatall brond:
Lo where the dreadfull Death behynd thy backe doth stond!'

XXXVIII
With that he strooke, and thother strooke withall,
That nothing seemd mote beare so monstrous might:
The one upon his covered shield did fall,
And glauncing downe would not his owner byte:
But th' other did upon his troncheon smyte,
Which hewing quite a sunder, further way
It made, and on his hacqueton did lyte,
The which dividing with importune sway,
It seizd in his right side, and there the dint did stay.

XXXIX
Wyde was the wound, and a large lukewarme flood,
Red as the rose, thence gushed grievously,
That when the Paynym spyde the streaming blood,
Gave him great hart, and hope of victory.
On thother side, in huge perplexity
The Prince now stood, having his weapon broke;
Nought could he hurt, but still at warde did ly:
Yet with his troncheon he so rudely stroke
Cymochles twise, that twise him forst his foot revoke.

XL
Whom when the palmer saw in such distresse,
Sir Guyons sword he lightly to him raught,
And said: 'Fayre sonne, great God thy right hand blesse,
To use that sword so well as he it ought.'
Glad was the knight, and with fresh courage fraught,
When as againe he armed felt his hond:
Then like a lyon, which hath long time saught
His robbed whelpes, and at the last them fond
Emongst the shepeheard swaynes, then wexeth wood and yond;

XLI
So fierce he laid about him, and dealt blowes
On either side, that neither mayle could hold,
Ne shield defend the thunder of his throwes:
Now to Pyrochles many strokes he told;

Eft to Cymochles twise so many fold:
Then backe againe turning his busie hond,
Them both atonce compeld with courage bold,
To yield wide way to his hart-thrilling brond;
And though they both stood stiffe, yet could not both withstond.

XLII
As salvage bull, whom two fierce mastives bayt,
When rancour doth with rage him once engore,
Forgets with wary warde them to awayt,
But with his dreadfull hornes them drives afore,
Or flings aloft, or treades downe in the flore,
Breathing out wrath, and bellowing disdaine,
That all the forest quakes to heare him rore:
So rag'd Prince Arthur twixt his foemen twaine,
That neither could his mightie puissaunce sustaine.

XLIII
But ever at Pyrochles when he smitt,
Who Guyons shield cast ever him before,
Whereon the Faery Queenes pourtract was writt,
His hand relented, and the stroke forbore,
And his deare hart the picture gan adore;
Which oft the Paynim sav'd from deadly stowre.
But him henceforth the same can save no more;
For now arrived is his fatall howre,
That no'te avoyded be by earthly skill or powre.

XLIV
For when Cymochles saw the fowle reproch,
Which them appeached, prickt with guiltie shame
And inward griefe, he fiercely gan approch,
Resolv'd to put away that loathly blame,
Or dye with honour and desert of fame;
And on the haubergh stroke the Prince so sore,
That quite disparted all the linked frame,
And pierced to the skin, but bit no more,
Yet made him twise to reele, that never moov'd afore.

XLV
Whereat renfierst with wrath and sharp regret,
He stroke so hugely with his borrowd blade,
That it empierst the Pagans burganet,
And cleaving the hard steele, did deepe invade
Into his head, and cruell passage made
Quite through his brayne. He, tombling downe on ground,
Breathd out his ghost, which, to th' infernall shade
Fast flying, there eternall torment found
For all the sinnes wherewith his lewd life did abound.

XLVI

Which when his german saw, the stony feare
Ran to his hart, and all his sence dismayd,
Ne thenceforth life ne corage did appeare;
But as a man, whom hellish feendes have frayd,
Long trembling still he stoode: at last thus sayd:
'Traytour, what hast hou doen? How ever may
Thy cursed hand so cruelly have swayd
Against that knight? Harrow and well away!
After so wicked deede why liv'st thou lenger day?'

XLVII
With that all desperate, as loathing light,
And with revenge desyring soone to dye,
Assembling all his force and utmost might,
With his owne swerd he fierce at him did flye,
And strooke, and foynd, and lasht outrageously,
Withouten reason or regard. Well knew
The Prince, with pacience and sufferaunce sly
So hasty heat soone cooled to subdew:
Tho, when this breathlesse woxe, that batteil gan renew.

XLVIII
As when a windy tempest bloweth hye,
That nothing may withstand his stormy stowre,
The clowdes, as thinges affrayd, before him flye;
But all so soone as his outrageous powre
Is layd, they fiercely then begin to showre,
And, as in scorne of his spent stormy spight,
Now all attonce their malice forth do poure:
So did Prince Arthur beare himselfe in fight,
And suffred rash Pyrochles waste his ydle might.

XLIX
At last when as the Sarazin perceiv'd,
How that straunge sword refusd to serve his neede,
But, when he stroke most strong, the dint deceiv'd,
He flong it from him, and, devoyd of dreed,
Upon him lightly leaping without heed,
Twixt his two mighty armes engrasped fast,
Thinking to overthrowe and downe him tred:
But him in strength and skill and Prince surpast,
And through his nimble sleight did under him down cast.

L
Nought booted it the Paynim then to strive;
For as a bittur in the eagles clawe,
That may not hope by flight to scape alive,
Still waytes for death with dread and trembling aw,
So he, now subject to the victours law,
Did not once move, nor upward cast his eye,
For vile disdaine and rancour, which did gnaw

His hart in twaine with sad melancholy,
As one that loathed life, and yet despysd to dye.

LI
But full of princely bounty and great mind,
The conquerour nought cared him to slay,
But casting wronges and all revenge behind,
More glory thought to give life then decay,
And sayd: 'Paynim, this is thy dismall day;
Yet if thou wilt renounce thy miscreaunce,
And my trew liegeman yield thy selfe for ay,
Life will I graunt thee for thy valiaunce,
And all thy wronges will wipe out of my sovenaunce.'

LII
'Foole!' sayd the Pagan, 'I thy gift defye;
But use thy fortune, as it doth befall,
And say, that I not overcome doe dye,
But in despight of life for death doe call.'
Wroth was the Prince, and sory yet withall,
That he so wilfully refused grace;
Yet, sith his fate so cruelly did fall,
His shining helmet he gan soone unlace,
And left his headlesse body bleeding all the place.

LIII
By this, Sir Guyon from his traunce awakt,
Life having maystered her sencelesse foe;
And looking up, when as his shield he lakt,
And sword saw not, he wexed wondrous woe:
But when the palmer, whom he long ygoe
Had lost, he by him spyde, right glad he grew,
And saide: 'Deare sir, whom wandring to and fro
I long have lackt, I joy thy face to vew:
Firme is thy faith, whom daunger never fro me drew.

LIV
'But read, what wicked hand hath robbed mee
Of my good sword and shield?' The palmer, glad
With so fresh hew uprysing him to see,
Him answered: 'Fayre sonne, be no whit sad
For want of weapons; they shall soone be had.'
So gan he to discourse the whole debate,
Which that straunge knight for him sustained had,
And those two Sarazins confounded late,
Whose carcases on ground were horribly prostrate.

LV
Which when he heard, and saw the tokens trew,
His hart with great affection was embayd,
And to the Prince bowing with reverence dew,

As to the patrone of his life, thus sayd:
'My lord, my liege, by whose most gratious ayd
I live this day, and see my foes subdewd,
What may suffise to be for meede repayd
Of so great graces as ye have me shewd,
But to be ever bound—'

LVI
To whom the infant thus: 'Fayre sir, what need
Good turnes be counted, as a servile bond,
To bind their dooers to receive their meed?
Are not all knightes by oath bound to withstond
Oppressours powre by armes and puissant hond?
Suffise, that i have done my dew in place.'
So goodly purpose they together fond
Of kindnesse and of courteous aggrace;
The whiles false Archimage and Atin fled aopace.

CANTO IX

The House of Temperance, in which
Doth sober Alma dwell,
Besiegd of many foes, whom straunger
Knightes to flight compell.

I
Of all Gods workes, which doe this world adorne,
There is no one more faire and excellent,
Then is mans body both for powre and forme,
Whiles it is kept in sober government;
But none then it more fowle and indecent,
Distempred through misrule and passions bace:
It growes a monster, and incontinent
Doth loose his dignity and native grace.
Behold, who list, both one and other in this place.

II
After the Paynim brethren conquer'd were,
The Briton Prince recov'ring his stolne sword,
And Guyon his lost shield, they both yfere
Forth passed on their way in fayre accord,
Till him the Prince with gentle court did bord:
'Sir knight, mote I of you this court'sy read,
To weet why on your shield, so goodly scord,
Beare ye the picture of that ladies head?
Full lively is the semblaunt, though the substance dead.'

III
'Fayre sir,' sayd he, 'if in that picture dead
Such life ye read, and vertue in vaine shew,
What mote ye weene, if the trew lively-head
Of that most glorious visage ye did vew?
But yf the beauty of her mind ye knew,
That is, her bounty and imperiall powre,
Thousand times fairer then her mortal hew,
O how great wonder would your thoughts devoure,
And infinite desire into your spirite poure!

IV
'Shee is the mighty Queene of Faery,
Whose faire retraitt I in my shield doe beare;
Shee is the flowre of grace and chastity,
Throughout the world renowmed far and neare,
My liefe, my liege, my soveraine, my deare,
Whose glory shineth as the morning starre,
And with her light the earth enlumines cleare:
Far reach her mercies, and her praises farre,
As well in state of peace, as puissaunce in warre.'

V
'Thrise happy man,' said then the Briton knight,
'Whom gracious lott and thy great valiaunce
Have made thee soldier of that princesse bright,
Which with her bounty and glad countenaunce
Doth blesse her servaunts, and them high advaunce.
How may straunge knight hope ever to aspire,
By faithfull service and meete amenaunce,
Unto such blisse? Sufficient were that hire
For losse of thousand lives, to die at her desire.'

VI
Said Guyon, 'Noble lord, what meed so great,
Or grace of earthly prince so soveraine,
But by your wondrous worth and warlike feat
Ye well may hope, and easely attaine?
But were your will, her sold to entertaine,
And numbred be mongst Knights of May-denhed,
Great guerdon, well I wote, should you remaine,
And in her favor high bee reckoned,
As Arthegall and Sophy now beene honored.'

VII
'Certes,' then said the Prince, 'I God avow,
That sith I armes and knighthood first did plight,
My whole desire hath beene, and yet is now,
To serve that Queene with al my powre and might.
Now hath the sunne with his lamp-burning light
Walkt round about the world, and I no lesse,

Sith of that goddesse I have sought the sight,
Yet no where can her find: such happinesse
Heven doth to me envy, and Fortune favourlesse.'

VIII
'Fortune, the foe of famous chevisaunce,
Seldome,' said Guyon, 'yields to vertue aide,
But in her way throwes mischiefe and mischaunce,
Whereby her course is stopt and passage staid.
But you, faire sir, be not herewith dismaid,
But constant keepe the way in which ye stand;
Which were it not that I am els delaid
With hard adventure, which I have in hand,
I labour would to guide you through al Fary Land.'

IX
'Gramercy, sir,' said he; 'but mote I weete
What straunge adventure doe ye now pursew?
Perhaps my succour or advizement meete
Mote stead you much your purpose to subdew.'
Then gan Sir Guyon all the story shew
Of false Acrasia, and her wicked wiles,
Which to avenge, the palmer him forth drew
From Faery court. So talked they, the whiles
They wasted had much way, and measurd many miles.

X
And now faire Phoebus gan decline in haste
His weary wagon to the westerne vale,
Whenas they spide a goodly castle, plaste
Foreby a river in a pleasaunt dale;
Which choosing for that evenings hospitale,
They thether marcht: but when they came in sight,
And from their sweaty coursers did avale,
They found the gates fast barred long ere night,
And every loup fast lockt, as fearing foes despight.

XI
Which when they saw, they weened fowle reproch
Was to them doen, their entraunce to forstall,
Till that the squire gan nigher to approch,
And wind his horne under the castle wall,
That with the noise it shooke, as it would fall.
Eftsoones forth looked from the highest spire
The watch, and lowd unto the knights did call,
To weete what they so rudely did require:
Who gently answered, they entraunce did desire.

XII
'Fly, fly, good knights,' said he, 'fly fast away,
If that your lives ye love, as meete ye should;

Fly fast, and save your selves from neare decay;
Here may ye not have entraunce, though we would:
We would and would againe, if that we could;
But thousand enemies about us rave,
And with long siege us in this castle hould:
Seven yeares this wize they us besieged have,
And many good knights slaine, that have us sought to save.'

XIII
Thus as he spoke, loe! with outragious cry
A thousand villeins rownd about them swarmd
Out of the rockes and caves adjoyning nye:
Vile caitive wretches, ragged, rude, deformd,
All threatning death, all in straunge manner armd;
Some with unweldy clubs, some with long speares,
Some rusty knifes, some staves in fier warmd.
Sterne was their looke, like wild amazed steares,
Staring with hollow eies, and stiffe upstanding heares.

XIV
Fiersly at first those knights they did assayle,
And drove them to recoile: but, when againe
They gave fresh charge, their forces gan to fayle,
Unhable their encounter to sustaine;
For with such puissaunce and impetuous maine
Those champions broke on them, that forst them fly,
Like scattered sheepe, whenas the shepherds swaine
A lyon and a tigre doth espye,
With greedy pace forth rushing from the forest nye.

XV
A while they fled, but soone retournd againe
With greater fury then before was fownd;
And evermore their cruell capitaine
Sought with his raskall routs t' enclose them rownd,
And overronne to tread them to the grownd.
But soone the knights with their bright-burning blades
Broke their rude troupes, and orders did confownd,
Hewing and slashing at their idle shades;
For though they bodies seem, yet substaunce from them fades.

XVI
As when a swarme of gnats at eventide
Out of the fennes of Allan doe arise,
Their murmuring small trompetts sownden wide,
Whiles in the aire their clustring army flies,
That as a cloud doth seeme to dim the skies;
Ne man nor beast may rest, or take repast,
For their sharpe wounds and noyous injuries,
Till the fierce northerne wind with blustring blast
Doth blow them quite away, and in the ocean cast.

XVII

Thus when they had that troublous rout disperst,
Unto the castle gate they come againe,
And entraunce crav'd, which was denied erst.
Now when report of that their perlous paine,
And combrous conflict which they did sustaine,
Came to the ladies eare, which there did dwell,
Shee forth issewed with a goodly traine
Of squires and ladies equipaged well,
And entertained them right fairely, as befell.

XVIII

Alma she called was, a virgin bright,
That had not yet felt Cupides wanton rage;
Yet was shee wooed of many a gentle knight,
And many a lord of noble parentage,
That sought with her to lincke in marriage,
For shee was faire, as faire mote ever bee,
And in the flowre now of her freshest age;
Yet full of grace and goodly modestee,
That even heven rejoyced her sweete face to see.

XIX

In robe of lilly white she was arayd,
That from her shoulder to her heele downe raught;
The traine whereof loose far behind her strayd,
Braunched with gold and perle, most richly wrought,
And borne of two faire damsels, which were taught
That service well. Her yellow golden heare
Was trimly woven, and in tresses wrought,
Ne other tire she on her head did weare,
But crowned with a garland of sweete rosiere.

XX

Goodly shee entertaind those noble knights,
And brought them up into her castle hall;
Where gentle court and gracious delight
Shee to them made, with mildnesse virginall,
Shewing her selfe both wise and liberall.
There when they rested had a season dew,
They her besought, of favour speciall,
Of that faire castle to affoord them vew:
Shee graunted, and them leading forth, the same did shew.

XXI

First she them led up to the castle wall,
That was so high as foe might not it clime,
And all so faire and fensible withall;
Not built of bricke, ne yet of stone and lime,
But of thing like to that Ægyptian slime,

Whereof King Nine whilome built Babell towre:
But O great pitty that no lenger time
So goodly workemanship should not endure!
Soone it must turne to earth: no earthly thing is sure.

XXII
The frame thereof seemd partly circulare,
And part triangulare: O worke divine!
Those two the first and last proportions are;
The one imperfect, mortall, fœminine,
Th' other immortall, perfect, masculine:
And twixt them both a quadrate was the base,
Proportioned equally by seven and nine;
Nine was the circle sett in heavens place:
All which compacted made a goodly diapase.

XXIII
Therein two gates were placed seemly well:
The one before, by which all in did pas,
Did th' other far in workmanship excell;
For not of wood, nor of enduring bras,
But of more worthy substance fram'd it was:
Doubly disparted, it did locke and close,
That, when it locked, none might thorough pas,
And when it opened, no man might it close;
Still open to their friendes, and closed to their foes.

XXIV
Of hewen stone the porch was fayrely wrought,
Stone more of valew, and more smooth and fine,
Then jett or marble far from Ireland brought;
Over the which was cast a wandring vine,
Enchaced with a wanton yvie twine.
And over it a fayre portcullis hong,
Which to the gate directly did incline,
With comely compasse and compacture strong,
Nether unseemly short, nor yet exceeding long.

XXV
Within the barbican a porter sate,
Day and night duely keeping watch and ward;
Nor wight nor word mote passe out of the gate,
But in good order, and with dew regard:
Utterers of secrets he from thence debard,
Bablers of folly, and blazers of cryme:
His larumbell might lowd and wyde be hard,
When cause requyrd, but never out of time;
Early and late it rong, at evening and at prime.

XXVI
And rownd about the porch on every syde

Twise sixteene warders satt, all armed bright
In glistring steele, and strongly fortifyde:
Tall yeomen seemed they, and of great might,
And were enraunged ready still for fight.
By them as Alma passed with her guestes,
They did obeysaunce, as beseemed right,
And then againe retourned to their restes:
The porter eke to her did lout with humble gestes.

XXVII
Thence she them brought into a stately hall,
Wherein were many tables fayre dispred
And ready dight with drapets festivall,
Against the viaundes should be ministred
At th' upper end there sate, yclad in red
Downe to the ground, a comely personage,
That in his hand a white rod menaged:
He steward was, hight Diet; rype of age,
And in demeanure sober, and in counsell sage.

XXVIII
And through the hall there walked to and fro
A jolly yeoman, marshall of the same,
Whose name was Appetite: he did bestow
Both guestes and meate, when ever in they came,
And knew them how to order without blame,
As him the steward badd. They both attone
Did dewty to their lady, as became;
Who, passing by, forth ledd her guestes anone
Into the kitchin rowme, ne spard for nicenesse none.

XXIX
It was a vaut ybuilt for great dispence,
With many raunges reard along the wall,
And one great chimney, whose long tonnell thence
The smoke forth threw: and in the midst of all
There placed was a caudron wide and tall,
Upon a mightie fornace, burning whott,
More whott then Aetn', or flaming Mongiball:
For day and night it brent, ne ceased not,
So long as any thing it in the caudron gott.

XXX
But to delay the heat, least by mischaunce
It might breake out, and set the whole on fyre,
There added was by goodly ordinaunce
An huge great payre of bellowes, which did styre
Continually, and cooling breath inspyre.
About the caudron many cookes accoyld,
With hookes and ladles, as need did requyre:
The whyles the viaundes in the vessell boyld,

They did about their businesse sweat, and sorely toyld.

XXXI
The maister cooke was cald Concoction,
A carefull man, and full of comely guyse.
The kitchin clerke, that hight Digestion,
Did order all th' achates in seemely wise,
And set them forth, as well he could devise.
The rest had severall offices assynd:
Some to remove the scum, as it did rise;
Others to beare the same away did mynd;
And others it to use according to his kynd.

XXXII
But all the liquour, which was fowle and waste,
Not good nor serviceable elles for ought,
They in another great rownd vessel plaste,
Till by a conduit pipe it thence were brought:
And all the rest, that noyous was and nought,
By secret wayes, that none might it espy,
Was close convaid, and to the backgate brougt,
That cleped was Port Esquiline, whereby
It was avoided quite, and throwne out privily.

XXXIII
Which goodly order and great workmans skill
Whenas those knightes beheld, with rare delight
And gazing wonder they their mindes did fill;
For never had they seene so straunge a sight.
Thence backe againe faire Alma led them right,
And soone into a goodly parlour brought,
That was with royall arras richly dight,
In which was nothing pourtrahed nor wrought,
Not wrought nor pourtrahed, but easie to be thought.

XXXIV
And in the midst thereof upon the floure,
A lovely bevy of faire ladies sate,
Courted of many a jolly paramoure,
The which them did in modest wise amate,
And eachone sought his lady to aggrate:
And eke emongst them litle Cupid playd
His wanton sportes, being retourned late
From his fierce warres, and having from him layd
His cruel bow, wherewith he thousands hath dismayd.

XXXV
Diverse delights they fownd them selves to please;
Some song in sweet consort, some laught for joy,
Some plaid with strawes, some ydly satt at ease;
But other some could not abide to toy,

All pleasaunce was to them griefe and annoy:
This frownd, that faund, the third for shame did blush,
Another seemed envious, or coy,
Another in her teeth did gnaw a rush:
But at these straungers presence every one did hush.

XXXVI
Soone as the gracious Alma came in place,
They all attonce out of their seates arose,
And to her homage made, with humble grace:
Whom when the knights beheld, they gan dispose
Themselves to court, and each a damzell chose.
The Prince by chaunce did on a lady light,
That was right faire and fresh as morning rose,
But somwhat sad and solemne eke in sight,
As if some pensive thought constraind her gentle spright.

XXXVII
In a long purple pall, whose skirt with gold
Was fretted all about, she was arayd;
And in her hand a poplar braunch did hold:
To whom the Prince in courteous maner sayd:
'Gentle madame, why beene ye thus dismayd,
And your faire beautie doe with sadnes spill?
Lives any, that you hath thus ill apayd?
Or doen you love, or doen you lack your will?
What ever bee the cause, it sure beseemes you ill.'

XXXVIII
'Fayre sir,' said she, halfe in disdainefull wise,
'How is it, that this word in me ye blame,
And in your selfe doe not the same advise?
Him ill beseemes, anothers fault to name,
That may unwares bee blotted with the same:
Pensive I yeeld I am, and sad in mind,
Through great desire of glory and of fame;
Ne ought I weene are ye therein behynd,
That have twelve moneths sought one, yet no where can her find.'

XXXIX
The Prince was inly moved at her speach,
Well weeting trew what she had rashly told,
Yet with faire semblaunt sought to hyde the breach,
Which chaunge of colour did perfoce unfold,
Now seeming flaming whott, now stony cold.
Tho, turning soft aside, he did inquyre
What wight she was, that poplar braunch did hold:
It answered was, her name was Praysdesire,
That by well doing sought to honour to aspyre.

XL

The whyles, the Faery knight did entertayne
Another damsell of that gentle crew,
That was right fayre, and modest of demayne,
But that too oft she chaung'd her native hew:
Straunge was her tyre, and all her garment blew,
Close rownd about her tuckt with many a plight:
Upon her fist the bird, which shonneth vew
And keepes in coverts close from living wight,
Did sitt, as yet ashamd, how rude Pan did her dight.

XLI
So long as Guyon with her commoned,
Unto the grownd she cast her modest eye,
And ever and anone with rosy red
The bashfull blood her snowy cheekes did dye,
That her became, as polisht yvory
Which cunning craftesman hand hath overlayd
With fayre vermilion or pure castory.
Great wonder had the knight, to see the mayd
So straungely passioned, and to her gently said:

XLII
'Fayre damzell, seemeth by your troubled cheare,
That either me too bold ye weene, this wise
You to molest, or other ill to feare
That in the secret of your hart close lyes,
From whence it doth, as cloud from sea, aryse.
If it be I, of pardon I you pray;
But if ought else that I mote not devyse,
I will, if please you it discure, assay
To ease you of that ill, so wisely as I may.'

XLIII
She answerd nought, but more abasht for shame,
Held downe her head, the whiles her lovely face
The flashing blood with blushing did inflame,
And the strong passion mard her modest grace,
That Guyon mervayld at her uncouth cace;
Till Alma him bespake: 'Why wonder yee,
Faire sir, at that which ye so much embrace?
She is the fountaine of your modestee;
You shamefast are, but Shamefastnes it selfe is shee.'

XLIV
Thereat the Elfe did blush in privitee,
And turnd his face away; but she the same
Dissembled faire, and faynd to oversee.
Thus they awhile with court and goodly game
Themselves did solace each one with his dame,
Till that great lady thence away them sought,
To vew her castles other wondrous frame.

Up to a stately turret she them brought,
Ascending by ten steps of alablaster wrought.

XLV
That turrets frame most admirable was,
Like highest heaven compassed around,
And lifted high above this earthly masse,
Which it survewd, as hils doen lower ground:
But not on ground mote like to this be found;
Not that, which antique Cadmus whylome built
In Thebes, which Alexander did confound;
Nor that proud towre of Troy, though richly guilt,
From which young Hectors blood by cruell Greekes was spilt.

XLVI
The roofe hereof was arched over head,
And deckt with flowers and herbars daintily:
Two goodly beacons, set in watches stead,
Therein gave light, and flamd continually;
For they of living fire most subtilly
Were made, and set in silver sockets bright,
Cover'd with lids deviz'd of substance sly,
That readily they shut and open might.
O who can tell the prayses of that makers might?

XLVII
Ne can I tell, ne can I stay to tell
This parts great workemanship and wondrous powre,
That all this other worldes worke doth excell,
And likest is unto that heavenly towre,
That God hath built for his owne blessed bowre.
Therein were divers rowmes, and divers stages,
But three the chiefest, and of greatest powre,
In which there dwelt three honorable sages,
The wisest men, I weene, that lived in their ages.

XLVIII
Not he, whom Greece, the nourse of all good arts,
By Phæbus doome, the wisest thought alive,
Might be compar'd to these by many parts:
Nor that sage Pylian syre, which did survive
Three ages, such as mortall men contrive,
By whose advise old Priams cittie fell,
With these in praise of pollicies mote strive.
These three in these three rowmes did sondry dwell,
And counselled faire Alma, how to governe well.

XLIX
The first of them could things to come foresee;
The next could of thinges present best advize;
The third things past could keepe in memoree:

So that no time nor reason could arize,
But that the same could one of these comprize.
Forthy the first did in the forepart sit,
That nought mote hinder his quicke prejudize:
He had a sharpe foresight, and working wit,
That never idle was, ne once would rest a whit.

L
His chamber was dispainted all with in
With sondry colours, in the which were writ
Infinite shapes of thinges dispersed thin;
Some such as in the world were never yit,
Ne can devized be of mortall wit;
Some daily seene, and knowen by their names,
Such as in idle fantasies doe flit:
Infernall hags, centaurs, feendes, hippodames,
Apes, lyons, aegles, owles, fooles, lovers, children, dames.

LI
And all the chamber filled was with flyes,
Which buzzed all about, and made such sound,
That they encombred all mens eares and eyes,
Like many swarmes of bees assembled round,
After their hives with honny do abound:
All those were idle thoughtes and fantasies,
Devices, dreames, opinions unsound,
Shewes, visions, sooth-sayes, and prophesies;
And all that fained is, as leasings, tales, and lies.

LII
Emongst them all sate he which wonned there,
That hight Phantastes by his nature trew,
A man of yeares yet fresh, as mote appere,
Of swarth complexion, and of crabbed hew,
That him full of melancholy did shew;
Bent hollow beetle browes, sharpe staring eyes,
That mad or foolish seemd: one by his vew
Mote deeme him borne with ill-disposed skyes,
When oblique Saturne sate in the house of agonyes.

LIII
Whom Alma having shewed to her guestes,
Thence brought them to the second rowme, whose wals
Were painted faire with memorable gestes
Of famous wisards, and with picturals
Of magistrates, of courts, of tribunals,
Of commen wealthes, of states, of pollicy,
Of lawes, of judgementes, and of decretals;
All artes, all science, all philosophy,
And all that in the world was ay thought wittily.

LIV
Of those that rowme was full, and them among
There sate a man of ripe and perfect age,
Who did them meditate all his life long,
That through continuall practise and usage,
He now was growne right wise and wondrous sage.
Great pleasure had those straunger knightes, to see
His goodly reason and grave personage,
That his disciples both desyrd to bee;
But Alma thence them led to th' hindmost rowme of three.

LV
That chamber seemed ruinous and old,
And therefore was removed far behind,
Yet were the wals, that did the same uphold,
Right firme and strong, though somwhat they declind;
And therein sat an old old man, halfe blind,
And all decrepit in his feeble corse,
Yet lively vigour rested in his mind,
And recompenst him with a better scorse:
Weake body well is chang'd for minds redoubled forse.

LVI
This man of infinite remembraunce was,
And things foregone through many ages held,
Which he recorded still, as they did pas,
Ne suffred them to perish through long eld,
As all things els, the which this world doth weld,
But laid them up in his immortall scrine,
Where they for ever incorrupted dweld:
The warres he well remembred of King Nine,
Of old Assaracus, and Inachus divine.

LVII
The yeares of Nestor nothing were to his,
Ne yet Mathusalem, though longest liv'd;
For he remembred both their infancis:
Ne wonder then, if that he were depriv'd
Of native strength now that he them surviv'd.
His chamber all was hangd about with rolls,
And old records from auncient times derivd,
Some made in books, some in long parchment scrolls,
That were all worm-eaten and full of canker holes.

LVIII
Amidst them all he in a chaire was sett,
Tossing and turning them withouten end;
But for he was unhable them to fett,
A litle boy did on him still attend,
To reach, when ever he for ought did send;
And oft when thinges were lost, or laid amis,

That boy them sought and unto him did lend:
Therefore he Anamnestes cleped is,
And that old man Eumnestes, by their propertis.

LIX
The knightes, there entring, did him reverence dew,
And wondred at his endlesse exercise.
Then as they gan his library to vew,
And antique regesters for to avise,
There chaunced to the Princes hand to rize
An aunciient booke, hight Briton Moniments,
That of this lands first conquest did devize,
And old division into regiments,
Till it reduced was to one mans governements.

LX
Sir Guyon chaunst eke on another booke,
That hight Antiquitee of Faery Lond:
In which whenas he greedily did looke,
Th' ofspring of Elves and Faryes there he fond,
As it delivered was from hond to hond.
Whereat they, burning both with fervent fire
Their countreys auncestry to understand,
Crav'd leave of Alma and that aged sire,
To read those bookes; who gladly graunted their desire.

CANTO X

A chronicle of Briton kings,
From Brute to Uthers rayne;
And rolls of Elfin emperours,
Till time of Gloriane.

I
Who now shall give unto me words and sound,
Equall unto this haughty enterprise?
Or who shall lend me wings, with which from ground
My lowly verse may loftily arise,
And lift it selfe unto the highest skyes?
More ample spirit, then hetherto was wount,
Here needes me, whiles the famous auncestryes
Of my most dreaded Soveraigne I recount,
By which all earthly princes she doth far surmount.

II
Ne under sunne, that shines so wide and faire,
Whence all that lives does borrow life and light,

Lives ought that to her linage may compaire,
Which, though from earth it be derived right,
Yet doth it selfe stretch forth to hevens hight,
And all the world with wonder overspred;
A labor huge, exceeding far my might:
How shall fraile pen, with feare disparaged,
Conceive such soveraine glory, and great bountyhed?

III
Argument worthy of Mœonian quill,
Or rather worthy of great Phoebus rote,
Whereon the ruines of great Ossa hill,
And triumphes of Phlegræan Jove, he wrote,
That all the gods admird his lofty note.
But, if some relish of that hevenly lay
His learned daughters would to me report,
To decke my song withall, I would assay
Thy name, O soveraine Queene, to blazon far away.

IV
Thy name, O soveraine Queene, thy realme, and race,
From this renowmed Prince derived arre,
Who mightily upheld that royall mace,
Which now thou bear'st, to thee descended farre
From mighty kings and conquerours in warre,
Thy fathers and great grandfathers of old,
Whose noble deeds above the northern starre
Immortall Fame for ever hath enrold;
As in that old mans booke they were in order told.

V
The land, which warlike Britons now possesse,
And therein have their mighty empire raysd,
In antique times was salvage wildernesse,
Unpeopled, unmannurd, unprovd, unpraysd;
Ne was it island then, ne was it paysd
Amid the ocean waves, ne was it sought
Of merchaunts farre, for profits therein praysd;
But was all desolate, and of some thought
By sea to have bene from the Celticke mayn-land brought.

VI
Ne did it then deserve a name to have,
Till that the venturous mariner that way,
Learning his ship from those white rocks to save,
Which all along the southerne sea-coast lay,
Threatning unheedy wrecke and rash decay,
For safeties sake that same his sea-marke made,
And namd it ALBION. But later day,
Finding in it fit ports for fishers trade,
Gan more the same frequent, and further to invade.

VII

But far in land a salvage nation dwelt
Of hideous giaunts, and halfe beastly men,
That never tasted grace, nor goodnes felt,
But like wild beastes lurking in loathsome den,
And flying fast as roebucke through the fen,
All naked without shame or care of cold,
By hunting and by spoiling liveden;
Of stature huge, and eke of corage bold,
That sonnes of men amazd their sternesse to behold.

VIII

But whence they sprong, or how they were begott,
Uneath is to assure; uneath to wene
That monstrous error, which doth some assott,
That Dioclesians fifty daughters shene
Into this land by chaunce have driven bene,
Where companing with feends and filthy sprights
Through vaine illusion of their lust unclene,
They brought forth geaunts, and such dreadful wights
As far exceeded men in their immeasurd mights.

IX

They held this land, and with their filthinesse
Polluted this same gentle soyle long time:
That their owne mother loathd their beastlinesse,
And gan abhorre her broods unkindly crime,
All were they borne of her owne native slime:
Until that Brutus, anciently deriv'd
From roiall stocke of old Assaracs line,
Driven by fatall error, here arriv'd,
And them of their unjust possession depriv'd.

X

But ere he had established his throne,
And spred his empire to the utmost shore,
He fought great batteils with his salvage fone;
In which he them defeated evermore,
And many giaunts left on groning flore,
That well can witnes yet unto this day
The westerne Hogh, besprincled with the gore
Of mighty Goëmot, whome in stout fray
Corineus conquered, and cruelly did slay.

XI

And eke that ample pitt, yet far renownd
For the large leape which Debon did compell
Coulin to make, being eight lugs of grownd,
Into the which retourning backe he fell:
But those three monstrous stones doe most excell

Which that huge sonne of hideous Albion,
Whose father Hercules in Fraunce did quell,
Great Godmer, threw, in fierce contention,
At bold Canutus; but of him was slaine anon.

XII

In meed of these great conquests by them gott,
Corineus had that province utmost west
To him assigned for his worthy lott,
Which of his name and memorable gest
He called Cornwaile, yet so called best:
And Debons shayre was that is Devonshyre:
But Canute had his portion from the rest,
The which he cald Canutium, for his hyre;
Now Cantium, which Kent we comenly inquyre.

XIII

Thus Brute this realme unto his rule subdewd,
And raigned long in great felicity,
Lov'd of his freends, and of his foes eschewd.
He left three sonnes, his famous progeny,
Borne of fayre Inogene of Italy;
Mongst whom he parted his imperiall state,
And Locrine left chiefe lord of Britany.
At last ripe age bad him surrender late
His life, and long good fortune, unto finall fate.

XIV

Locrine was left the soveraine lord of all;
But Albanact had all the northerne part,
Which of him selfe Albania he did call;
And Camber did possesse the westerne quart,
Which Severne now from Logris doth depart:
And each his portion peaceably enjoyd,
Ne was there outward breach, nor grudge in hart,
That once their quiet government annoyd,
But each his paynes to others profit still employd.

XV

Untill a nation straung, with visage swart
And corage fierce, that all men did affray,
Which through the world then swarmd in every part,
And overflow'd all countries far away,
Like Noyes great flood, with their importune sway,
This land invaded with like violence,
And did themselves through all the north display:
Untill that Locrine, for his realmes defence,
Did head against them make, and strong munificence.

XVI

He them encountred, a confused rout,

Foreby the river, that whylome was hight
The ancient Abus, where with courage stout
He them defeated in victorious fight,
And chaste so fiercely after fearefull flight,
That forst their chiefetain, for his safeties sake,
(Their chiefetain Humber named was aright,)
Unto the mighty streame him to betake,
Where he an end of batteill, and of life did make.

XVII
The king retourned proud of victory,
And insolent wox through unwonted ease,
That shortly he forgot the jeopardy,
Which in his land he lately did appease,
And fell to vaine voluptuous disease:
He lov'd faire Ladie Estrild, leudly lov'd,
Whose wanton pleasures him too much did please,
That quite his hart from Guendolene remov'd,
From Guendolene his wife, though alwaies faithful prov'd.

XVIII
The noble daughter of Corineus
Would not endure to bee so vile disdaind,
But, gathering force and corage valorous,
Encountred him in batteill well ordaind,
In which him vanquisht she to fly constraind:
But she so fast pursewd, that him she tooke,
And threw in bands, where he till death remaind:
Als his faire leman, flying through a brooke,
She overhent, nought moved with her piteous looke.

XIX
But both her selfe, and eke her daughter deare,
Begotten by her kingly paramoure,
The faire Sabrina, almost dead with feare,
She there attached, far from all succoure;
The one she slew in that impatient stoure,
But the sad virgin, innocent of all,
Adowne the rolling river she did poure,
Which of her name now Severne men do call:
Such was the end that to disloyall love did fall.

XX
Then, for her sonne, which she to Locrin bore,
Madan, was young, unmeet the rule to sway,
In her owne hand the crowne she kept in store,
Till ryper yeares he raught, and stronger stay:
During which time her powre she did display
Through all this realme, the glory of her sex,
And first taught men a woman to obay:
But when her sonne to mans estate did wex,

She it surrendred, ne her selfe would lenger vex.

XXI
Tho Madan raignd, unworthie of his race:
For with all shame that sacred throne he fild:
Next Memprise, as unworthy of that place,
In which being consorted with Manild,
For thirst of single kingdom him he kild.
But Ebranck salved both their infamies
With noble deedes, and warreyd on Brunchild
In Henault, where yet of his victories
Brave moniments remaine, which yet that land envies.

XXII
An happy man in his first dayes he was,
And happy father of faire progeny:
For all so many weekes as the yeare has,
So many children he did multiply;
Of which were twentie sonnes, which did apply
Their mindes to prayse and chevalrous desyre:
Those germans did subdew all Germany,
Of whom it hight; but in the end their syre
With foule repulse from Fraunce was forced to retyre.

XXIII
Which blott his sonne succeeding in his seat,
The second Brute, the second both in name
And eke in semblaunce of his puissaunce great,
Right well recur'd, and did away that blame
With recompence of everlasting fame.
He with his victour sword first opened
The bowels of wide Fraunce, a forlorne dame,
And taught her first how to be conquered;
Since which, with sondrie spoiles she hath bene ransacked.

XXIV
Let Scaldis tell, and let tell Hania,
And let the marsh of Esthambruges tell,
What colour were their waters that same day,
And all the moore twixt Elversham and Dell,
With blood of Henalois, which therein fell.
How oft that day did sad Brunchildis see
The greene shield dyde in dolorous vermell!
That not scuith guiridh it mote seeme to bee,
But rather y scuith gogh, signe of sad crueltee.

XXV
His sonne, King Leill, by fathers labour long,
Enjoyd an heritage of lasting peace,
And built Cairleill, and built Cairleon strong.
Next Huddibras his realme did not encrease,

But taught the land from wearie wars to cease.
Whose footsteps Bladud following, in artes
Exceld at Athens all the learned preace,
From whence he brought them to these salvage parts,
And with sweet science mollifide their stubborne harts.

XXVI
Ensample of his wondrous faculty,
Behold the boyling bathes at Cairbadon,
Which seeth with secret fire eternally,
And in their entrailles, full of quick brimston,
Nourish the flames which they are warmd upon,
That to their people wealth they forth do well,
And health to every forreyne nation:
Yet he at last, contending to excell
The reach of men, through flight into fond mischief fell.

XXVII
Next him King Leyr in happie peace long raynd,
But had no issue male him to succeed,
But three faire daughters, which were well uptraind
In all that seemed fitt for kingly seed:
Mongst whom his realme he equally decreed
To have divided. Tho, when feeble age
Nigh to his utmost date he saw proceed,
He cald his daughters, and with speeches sage
Inquyrd, which of them most did love her parentage.

XXVIII
The eldest Gonorill gan to protest,
That she much more then her owne life him lov'd;
And Regan greater love to him profest
Then all the world, when ever it were proov'd;
But Cordeill said she lov'd him as behoov'd:
Whose simple answere, wanting colours fayre
To paint it forth, him to displeasaunce moov'd,
That in his crown he counted her no hayre,
But twixt the other twain his kingdom whole did shayre.

XXIX
So wedded th' one to Maglan, king of Scottes,
And thother to the king of Cambria,
And twixt them shayrd his realme by equall lottes:
But without dowre the wise Cordelia
Was sent to aggannip of Celtica.
Their aged syre, thus eased of his crowne,
A private life ledd in Albania,
With Gonorill, long had in great renowne,
That nought him griev'd to beene from rule deposed downe.

XXX

But true it is that, when the oyle is spent,
The light goes out, and weeke is throwne away;
So when he had resignd his regiment,
His daughter gan despise his drouping day,
And wearie wax of his continuall stay.
Tho to his daughter Regan he repayrd,
Who him at first well used every way;
But when of his departure she despayrd,
Her bountie she abated, and his cheare empayrd.

XXXI

The wretched man gan then avise to late,
That love is not, where most it is profest;
Too truely tryde in his extremest state.
At last, resolv'd likewise to prove the rest,
He to Cordelia him selfe addrest,
Who with entyre affection him receav'd,
As for her syre and king her seemed best;
And after all an army strong she leav'd,
To war on those which him had of his realme bereav'd.

XXXII

So to his crowne she him restord againe,
In which he dyde, made ripe for death by eld,
And after wild, it should to her remaine:
Who peaceably the same long time did weld,
And all mens harts in dew obedience held:
Till that her sisters children, woxen strong,
Through proud ambition against her rebeld,
And overcommen kept in prison long,
Till, weary of that wretched life, her selfe she hong.

XXXIII

Then gan the bloody brethren both to raine:
But fierce Cundah gan shortly to envy
His brother Morgan, prickt with proud disdaine,
To have a pere in part of soverainty;
And kindling coles of cruell enmity,
Raisd warre, and him in batteill overthrew:
Whence as he to those woody hilles did fly,
Which hight of him Glamorgan, there him slew:
Then did he raigne alone, when he none equall knew.

XXXIV

His sonne Rivall' his dead rowme did supply,
In whose sad time blood did from heaven rayne:
Next great Gurgustus, then faire Cæcily,
In constant peace their kingdomes did contayne:
After whom Lago and Kinmarke did rayne,
And Gorbogud, till far in yeares he grew:
Then his ambitious sonnes unto them twayne

Arraught the rule, and from their father drew:
Stout Ferrex and sterne Porrex him in prison threw.

XXXV
But O! the greedy thirst of royall crowne,
That knowes no kinred, nor regardes no right,
Stird Porrex up to put his brother downe;
Who, unto him assembling forreigne might,
Made warre on him, and fell him selfe in fight:
Whose death t' avenge, his mother mercilesse,
Most mercilesse of women, Wyden hight,
Her other sonne fast sleeping did oppresse,
And with most cruell hand him murdred pittilesse.

XXXVI
Here ended Brutus sacred progeny,
Which had seven hundred yeares this scepter borne,
With high renowme and great felicity:
The noble braunch from th' antique stocke was torne
Through discord, and the roiall throne forlorne:
Thenceforth this realme was into factions rent,
Whilest each of Brutus boasted to be borne,
That in the end was left no moniment
Of Brutus, nor of Britons glorie auncient.

XXXVII
Then up arose a man of matchlesse might,
And wondrous wit to menage high affayres,
Who, stird with pitty of the stressed plight
Of this sad realme, cut into sondry shayres
By such as claymd themselves Brutes right-full hayres,
Gathered the princes of the people loose,
To taken counsell of their common cares;
Who, with his wisedom won, him streight did choose
Their king, and swore him fealty, to win or loose.

XXXVIII
Then made he head against his enimies,
And Ymner slew, of Logris miscreate;
Then Ruddoc and proud Stater, both allyes,
This of Albany newly nominate,
And that of Cambry king confirmed late,
He overthrew through his owne valiaunce;
Whose countries he redus'd to quiet state,
And shortly brought to civile governaunce,
Now one, which earst were many made through variaunce.

XXXIX
Then made he sacred lawes, which some men say
Were unto him reveald in vision,
By which he freed the traveilers high way,

The churches part, and ploughmans portion,
Restraining stealth and strong extortion;
The gratious Numa of Great Britany:
For, till his dayes, the chiefe dominion
By strength was wielded without pollicy;
Therefore he first wore crowne of gold for dignity.

XL
Donwallo dyde (for what may live for ay?)
And left two sonnes, of pearelesse prowesse both,
That sacked Rome too dearely did assay,
The recompence of their perjured oth,
And ransackt Greece wel tryde, when they were wroth;
Besides subjected France and Germany,
Which yet their praises speake, all be they loth,
And inly tremble at the memory
Of Brennus and Belinus, kinges of Britany.

XLI
Next them did Gurgunt, great Belinus sonne,
In rule succeede, and eke in fathers praise:
He Easterland subdewd, and Denmarke wonne,
And of them both did foy and tribute raise,
The which was dew in his dead fathers daies:
He also gave to fugitives of Spayne,
Whom he at sea found wandring from their waies,
A seate in Ireland safely to remayne,
Which they should hold of him, as subject to Britayne.

XLII
After him raigned Guitheline his hayre,
The justest man and trewest in his daies,
Who had to wife Dame Mertia the fayre,
A woman worthy of immortall praise,
Which for this realme found many goodly layes,
And wholesome statutes to her husband brought:
Her many deemd to have beene of the Fayes,
As was Aegerie, that Numa tought:
Those yet of her be Mertian lawes both nam'd and thought.

XLIII
Her sonne Sisillus after her did rayne,
And then Kimarus, and then Danius;
Next whom Morindus did the crowne sustayne,
Who, had he not with wrath outrageous
And cruell rancour dim'd his valorous
And mightie deedes, should matched have the best:
As well in that same field victorious
Against the forreine Morands he exprest:
Yet lives his memorie, though carcas sleepe in rest.

XLIV
Five sonnes he left begotten of one wife,
All which successively by turnes did rayne;
First Gorboman, a man of vertuous life;
Next Archigald, who, for his proud disdayne,
Deposed was from princedome soverayne,
And pitteous Elidure put in his sted;
Who shortly it to him restord agayne,
Till by his death he it recovered;
But Peridure and Vigent him disthronized.

XLV
In wretched prison long he did remaine,
Till they outraigned had their utmost date,
And then therein reseized was againe,
And ruled long with honorable state,
Till he surrendred realme and life to fate.
Then all the sonnes of these five brethren raynd
By dew successe, and all their nephewes late;
Even thrise eleven descents the crowne retaynd,
Till aged Hely by dew heritage it gaynd.

XLVI
He had two sonnes, whose eldest, called Lud,
Left of his life most famous memory,
And endlesse moniments of his great good:
The ruin'd wals he did reædifye
Of Troynovant, gainst force of enimy,
And built that gate which of his name is hight,
By which he lyes entombed solemnly.
He left two sonnes, too young to rule aright,
Androgeus and Tenantius, pictures of his might.

XLVII
Whilst they were young, Cassibalane their eme
Was by the people chosen in their sted,
Who on him tooke the roiall diademe,
And goodly well long time it governed;
Till the prowde Romanes him disquieted,
And warlike Cæsar, tempted with the name
Of this sweet island, never conquered,
And envying the Britons blazed fame,
(O hideous hunger of dominion!) hether came.

XLVIII
Yet twise they were repulsed backs againe,
And twise renforst backs to their ships to fly,
The whiles with blood they all the shore did staine,
And the gray ocean into purple dy:
Ne had they footing found at last perdie,
Had not Androgeus, false to native soyle,

And envious of uncles soveraintie,
Betrayd his countrey unto forreine spoyle:
Nought els but treason from the first this land did foyle.

XLIX
So by him Cæsar got the victory,
Through great bloodshed and many a sad assay,
In which himselfe was charged heavily
Of bardy Nennius, whom he yet did slay,
But lost his sword, yet to be seene this day.
Thenceforth this land was tributarie made
T'ambitious Rome, and did their rule obay,
Till Arthur all that reckoning defrayd;
Yet oft the Briton kings against them strongly swayd.

L
Next him Tenantius raignd; then Kimbeline,
What time th' Eternall Lord in fleshly slime
Enwombed was, from wretched Adams line
To purge away the guilt of sinfull crime:
O joyous memorie of happy time,
That heavenly grace so plenteously displayd!
O too high ditty for my simple rime!
Soone after this the Romanes him warrayd,
For that their tribute he refusd to let be payd.

LI
Good Claudius, that next was emperour,
An army brought, and with him batteile fought,
In which the king was by a treachetour
Disguised slaine, ere any thereof thought:
Yet ceased not the bloody fight for ought;
For Arvirage his brothers place supplyde,
Both in his armes and crowne, and by that draught
Did drive the Romanes to the weaker syde,
That they to peace agreed. So all was pacifyde.

LII
Was never king more highly magnifide,
Nor dredd of Romanes, then was Arvirage;
For which the emperour to him allide
His daughter Genuiss' in marriage:
Yet shortly he renounst the vassallage
Of Rome againe, who hether hastly sent
Vespasian, that with great spoile and rage
Forwasted all, till Genuissa gent
Persuaded him to ceasse, and her lord to relent.

LIII
He dide; and him succeeded Marius,
Who joyd his dayes in great tranquillity:

Then Coyll, and after him good Lucius,
That first received Christianity,
The sacred pledge of Christes Evangely:
Yet true it is, that long before that day
Hither came Joseph of Arimathy,
Who brought with him the Holy Grayle, (they say)
And preacht the truth; but since it greatly did decay.

LIV
This good king shortly without issew dide,
Whereof great trouble in the kingdome grew,
That did her selfe in sondry parts divide,
And with her powre her owne selfe overthrew,
Whilest Romanes daily did the weake subdew:
Which seeing stout Bunduca, up arose,
And taking armes, the Britons to her drew;
With whom she marched streight against her foes,
And them unwares besides the Severne did enclose.

LV
There she with them a cruell batteill tryde,
Not with so good successe as shee deserv'd,
By reason that the captaines on her syde,
Corrupted by Paulinus, from her swerv'd:
Yet such as were through former flight preserv'd
Gathering againe, her host she did renew,
And with fresh corage on the victor serv'd:
But being all defeated, save a few,
Rather then fly, or be captiv'd, her selfe she slew.

LVI
O famous moniment of womens prayse,
Matchable either to Semiramis,
Whom antique history so high doth rayse,
Or to Hypsiphil', or to Thomiris!
Her host two hundred thousand numbred is;
Who, whiles good fortune favoured her might,
Triumphed oft against her enemies;
And yet, though overcome in haplesse fight,
Shee triumphed on death, in enemies despight.

LVII
Her reliques Fulgent having gathered,
Fought with Severus, and him overthrew;
Yet in the chace was slaine of them that fled:
So made them victors whome he did subdew.
Then gan Carausius tirannize anew,
And gainst the Romanes bent their proper powre;
But him Allectus treacherously slew,
And tooke on him the robe of emperoure:
Nath'lesse the same enjoyed but short happy howre.

LVIII
For Asclepiodate him overcame,
And left inglorious on the vanquisht playne,
Without or robe or rag to hide his shame.
Then afterwards he in his stead did raigne;
But shortly was by Coyll in batteill slaine:
Who after long debate, since Lucies tyme,
Was of the Britons first crownd soveraine.
Then gan this realme renew her passed prime:
He of his name Coylchester built of stone and lime.

LIX
Which when the Romanes heard, they hether sent
Constantius, a man of mickle might,
With whome King Coyll made an agreement,
And to him gave for wife his daughter bright,
Fayre Helena, the fairest living wight;
Who in all godly thewes, and goodly praise,
Did far excell, but was most famous hight
For skil in musicke of all in her daies,
Aswell in curious instruments as cunning laies.

LX
Of whom he did great Constantine begett,
Who afterward was emperour of Rome;
To which whiles absent he his mind did sett,
Octavius here lept into his roome,
And it usurped by unrighteous doome:
But he his title justifide by might,
Slaying Traherne, and having overcome
The Romane legion in dreadfull fight:
So settled he his kingdome, and confirmd his right.

LXI
But wanting yssew male, his daughter deare
He gave in wedlocke to Maximian,
And him with her made of his kingdome heyre,
Who soone by meanes thereof the empire wan,
Till murdred by the freends of Gratian.
Then gan the Hunnes and Picts invade this land,
During the raigne of Maximinian;
Who dying left none heire them to withstand,
But that they overran all parts with easy hand.

LXII
The weary Britons, whose war-hable youth
Was by Maximian lately ledd away,
With wretched miseryes and woefull ruth
Were to those pagans made an open pray,
And daily spectacle of sad decay:

Whome Romane warres, which now fowr hundred yeares
And more had wasted, could no whit dismay;
Til by consent of Commons and of Peares,
They crownd the second Constantine with joyous teares.

LXIII
Who having oft in batteill vanquished
Those spoylefull Picts, and swarming Easterlings,
Long time in peace his realme established,
Yet oft annoyd with sondry bordragings
Of neighbour Scots, and forrein scatterlings,
With which the world did in those dayes abound:
Which to outbarre, with painefull pyonings
From sea to sea he heapt a mighty mound,
Which from Alcluid to Panwelt did that border bownd.

LXIV
Three sonnes he dying left, all under age;
By meanes whereof, their uncle Vortigere
Usurpt the crowne during their pupillage;
Which th' infants tutors gathering to feare,
Them closely into Armorick did beare:
For dread of whom, and for those Picts annoyes,
He sent to Germany, straunge aid to reare;
From whence eftsoones arrived here three hoyes
Of Saxons, whom he for his safety imployes.

LXV
Two brethren were their capitayns, which hight
Hengist and Horsus, well approv'd in warre,
And both of them men of renowmed might;
Who, making vantage of their civile jarre,
And of those forreyners which came from farre,
Grew great, and got large portions of land,
That in the realme ere long they stronger arre
Then they which sought at first their helping hand,
And Vortiger have forst the kingdome to aband.

LXVI
But by the helpe of Vortimere his sonne,
He is againe unto his rule restord;
And Hengist, seeming sad for that was donne,
Received is to grace and new accord,
Through his faire daughters face and flattring word.
Soone after which, three hundred lords he slew
Of British blood, all sitting at his bord;
Whose dolefull moniments who list to rew,
Th'eternall marks of treason may at Stonheng vew.

LXVII
By this the sonnes of Constantine, which fled,

Ambrose and Uther, did ripe yeares attayne,
And here arriving, strongly challenged
The crowne, which Vortiger did long detayne;
Who, flying from his fuilt, by them was slayne,
And Hengist eke soone brought to shamefull death.
Thenceforth Aurelius peaceably did rayne,
Till that throught poyson stopped was his breath;
So now entombed lies at Stoneheng by the heath.

LXVIII
After him Uther, which Pendragon hight,
Succeeding —— There abruptly it did end,
Without full point, or other cesure right,
As if the rest some wicked hand did rend,
Or th' author selfe could not at least attend
To finish it: that so untimely breach
The Prince him selfe halfe seemed to offend;
Yet secret pleasure did offence empeach,
And wonder of antiquity long stopt his speach.

LXIX
At last, quite ravisht with delight, to heare
The royall ofspring of his native land,
Gryde out: 'Deare countrey! O how dearely deare
Ought thy remembraunce and perpetual band
Be to thy foster childe, that from thy hand
Did commun breath and nouriture receave!
How brutish is it not to understand
How much to her we owe, that all us gave,
That gave unto us all, what ever good we have!'

LXX
But Guyon all this while his booke did read,
Ne yet has ended: for it was a great
And ample volume, that doth far excead
My leasure, so long leaves here to repeat:
It told, how first Prometheus did create
A man, of many parts from beasts deryv'd,
And then stole fire from heven, to animate
His worke, for which he was by Jove depryv'd
Of life him self, and hart-strings of an aegle ryv'd.

LXXI
That man so made he called Elfe, to weet
Quick, the first author of all Elfin kynd:
Who, wandring through the world with wearie feet,
Did in the gardins of Adonis fynd
A goodly creature, whom he deemd in mynd
To be no earthly wight, but either spright
Or angell, th' authour of all woman kynd;
Therefore a Fay he her according hight,

Of whom all Faryes spring, and fetch their lignage right.

LXXII
Of these a mighty people shortly grew,
And puissant kinges, which all the world warrayd,
And to them selves all nations did subdew.
The first and eldest, which that scepter swayd,
Was Elfin; him all India obayd,
And all that now America men call:
Next him was noble Elfinan, who laid
Cleopolis foundation first of all:
But Elfiline enclosd it with a golden wall.

LXXIII
His sonne was Elfinell, who overcame
The wicked Gobbelines in bloody field:
But Elfant was of most renowmed fame,
Who all of christall did Panthea build:
Then Elfar, who two brethren gyauntes kild,
The one of which had two heades, th' other three:
Then Elfinor, who was in magick skild;
He built by art upon the glassy see
A bridge of bras, whose sound hevens thunder seem'd to bee.

LXXIV
He left three sonnes, the which in order raynd,
And all their ofspring, in their dew descents,
Even seven hundred princes, which maintaynd
With mightie deedes their sondry governments;
That were too long their infinite contents
Here to record, ne much materiall;
Yet should they be most famous moniments,
And brave ensample, both of martiall
And civil rule, to kinges and states imperiall.

LXXV
After all these Elficleos did rayne,
The wise Elficleos in great majestie,
Who mightily that scepter did sustayne,
And with rich spoyles and famous victorie
Did high advaunce the crowne of Faery:
He left two sonnes, of which faire Elferon,
The eldest brother, did untimely dy;
Whose emptie place the mightie Oberon
Doubly supplide, in spousall and dominion.

LXXVI
Great was his power and glorie over all
Which, him before, that sacred seate did fill,
That yet remaines his wide memoriall:
He dying left the fairest Tanaquill,

Him to succeede therein, by his last will:
Fairer and nobler liveth none this howre,
Ne like in grace, ne like in learned skill;
Therefore they Glorian call that glorious flowre:
Long mayst thou, Glorian, live, in glory and great powre!

LXXVII
Beguyld thus with delight of novelties,
And naturall desire of countryes state,
So long they redd in those antiquities,
That how the time was fled they quite forgate;
Till gentle Alma, seeing it so late,
Perforce their studies broke, and them besought
To thinke how supper did them long awaite:
So halfe unwilling from their bookes them brought,
And fayrely feasted, as so noble knightes she ought.

CANTO XI

The enimies of Temperaunce
Besiege her dwelling place:
Prince Arthure them repelles, and fowle
Maleger doth deface.

I
What warre so cruel, or what siege so sore,
As that which strong affections doe apply
Against the forte of reason evermore,
To bring the sowle into captivity?
Their force is fiercer through infirmity
Of the fraile flesh, relenting to their rage,
And exercise most bitter tyranny
Upon the partes, brought into their bondage:
No wretchednesse is like to sinfull vellenage.

II
But in a body which doth freely yeeld
His partes to reasons rule obedient,
And letteth her, that ought, the scepter weeld,
All happy peace and goodly government
Is setled there in sure establishment.
There Alma, like a virgin queene most bright,
Doth florish in all beautie excellent,
And to her guestes doth bounteous banket dight,
Attempred goodly well for health and for delight.

III

Early, before the morne with cremosin ray
The windowes of bright heaven opened had,
Through which into the world the dawning day
Might looke, that maketh every creature glad,
Uprose Sir Guyon, in bright armour clad,
And to his purposd journey him prepar'd:
With him the palmer eke in habit sad
Him selfe addrest to that adventure hard:
So to the rivers syde they both together far'd.

IV
Where them awaited ready at the ford
The ferriman, as Alma had behight,
With his well rigged bote. They goe abord,
And he eftsoones gan launch his barke forth-right.
Ere long they rowed were quite out of sight,
And fast the land behynd them fled away.
But let them pas, whiles winde and wether right
Doe serve their turnes: here I a while must stay,
To see a cruell fight doen by the Prince this day.

V
For all so soone as Guyon thence was gon
Upon his voyage with his trustie guyde,
That wicked band of villeins fresh begon
That castle to assaile on every side,
And lay strong siege about it far and wyde.
So huge and infinite their numbers were,
That all the land they under them did hyde;
So fowle and ugly, that exceeding feare
Their visages imprest, when they approched neare.

VI
Them in twelve troupes their captein did dispart,
And round about in fittest steades did place,
Where each might best offend his proper part,
And his contrary object most deface,
As every one seem'd meetest in that cace.
Seven of the same against the castle gate
In strong entrenchments he did closely place,
Which with incessaunt force and endlesse hate
They battred day and night, and entraunce did awate.

VII
The other five, five sondry wayes he sett,
Against the five great bulwarkes of that pyle,
And unto each a bulwarke did arrett,
T' assayle with open force or hidden guyle,
In hope thereof to win victorious spoile.
They all that charge did fervently apply
With greedie malice and importune toyle,

And planted there their huge artillery,
With which they dayly made most dreadfull battery.

VIII
The first troupe was a monstrous rablement
Of fowle misshapen wightes, of which some were
Headed like owles, with beckes uncomely bent,
Others like dogs, others like gryphons dreare,
And some had wings, and some had clawes to teare,
And every one of them had lynces eyes,
And every one did bow and arrowes beare;
All those were lawlesse lustes, corrupt envyes,
And covetous aspects, all cruel enimyes.

IX
Those same against the bulwarke of the Sight
Did lay strong siege and battailous assault,
Ne once did yield it respitt day nor night,
But soone as Titan gan his head exault,
And soone againe as he his light withhault,
Their wicked engins they against it bent:
That is, each thing by which the eyes may fault:
But two, then all more huge and violent,
Beautie and money, they that bulwarke sorely rent.

X
The second bulwarke was the Hearing Sence,
Gainst which the second troupe dessignment makes,
Deformed creatures, in straunge difference,
Some having heads like harts, some like to snakes,
Some like wilde bores late rouzd out of the brakes;
Slaunderous reproches, and fowle infamies,
Leasinges, backbytinges, and vaineglorious crakes,
Bad counsels, prayses, and false flatteries;
All those against that fort did bend their batteries.

XI
Likewise that same third fort, that is the Smell,
Of that third troupe was cruelly assayd;
Whose hideous shapes were like to feendes of hell,
Some like to houndes, some like to apes, dismayd,
Some like to puttockes, all in plumes arayd;
All shap't according their conditions:
For by those ugly formes weren pourtrayd
Foolish delights and fond abusions,
Which doe that sence besiege with light illusions.

XII
And that fourth band, which cruell battry bent
Against the fourth bulwarke, that is the Taste,
Was, as the rest, a grysie rablement,

Some mouth'd like greedy oystriges, some faste
Like loathly toades, some fashioned in the waste
Like swine; for so deformd is luxury,
Surfeat, misdiet, and unthriftie waste,
Vaine feastes, and ydle superfluity:
All those this sences fort assayle incessantly.

XIII
But the fift troupe, most horrible of hew
And ferce of force, is dreadfull to report:
For some like snailes, some did like spyders shew,
And some like ugly urchins thick and short:
Cruelly they assayled that fift fort,
Armed with dartes of sensuall delight,
With stinges of carnall lust, and strong effort
Of feeling pleasures, with which day and night
Against that same fift bulwarke they continued fight.

XIV
Thus these twelve troupes with dreadfull puissaunce
Against that castle restlesse siege did lay,
And evermore their hideous ordinaunce
Upon the bulwarkes cruelly did play,
That now it gan to threaten neare decay;
And evermore their wicked capitayn
Provoked them the breaches to assay,
Somtimes with threats, somtimes with hope of gayn,
Which by the ransack of that peece they should attayn.

XV
On th' other syde, th' assieged castles ward
Their stedfast stonds did mightily maintaine,
And many bold repulse and many hard
Atchievement wrought, with perill and with payne,
That goodly frame from ruine to sustaine:
And those two brethren gyauntes did defend
The walles so stoutly with their sturdie mayne,
That never entraunce any durst pretend,
But they to direfull death their groning ghosts did send.

XVI
The noble virgin, ladie of the place,
Was much dismayed with that dreadful sight;
For never was she in so evill cace:
Till that the Prince, seeing her wofull plight,
Gan her recomfort from so sad affright,
Offring his service and his dearest life
For her defence, against that carle to fight,
Which was their chiefe and th' authour of that strife:
She him remercied as the patrone of her life.

XVII
Eftsoones himselfe in glitterand armes he dight,
And his well proved weapons to him hent:
So taking courteous conge, he behight
Those gates to be unbar'd, and forth he went.
Fayre mote he thee, the prowest and most gent
That ever brandished bright steele on hye:
Whom soone as that unruly rablement
With his gay squyre issewing did espye,
They reard a most outrageous dreadfull yelling cry;

XVIII
And therewithall attonce at him let fly
Their fluttring arrowes, thicke as flakes of snow,
And round about him flocke impetuously,
Like a great water flood, that, tombling low
From the high mountaines, threates to over-flow
With suddein fury all the fertile playne,
And the sad husbandmans long hope doth throw
A downe the streame, and all his vowes make vayne,
Nor bounds nor banks his headlong ruine may sustayne.

XIX
Upon his shield their heaped hayle he bore,
And with his sword disperst the raskall flockes,
Which fled a sonder, and him fell before,
As withered leaves drop from their dryed stockes,
When the wroth western wind does reave their locks;
And under neath him his courageous steed,
The fierce Spumador, trode them downe like docks;
The fierce Spumador borne of heavenly seed,
Such as Laomedon of Phæbus race did breed.

XX
Which suddeine horrour and confused cry
When as their capteine heard, in haste he yode,
The cause to weet, and fault to remedy:
Upon a tygre swift and fierce he rode,
That as the winde ran underneath his lode,
Whiles his long legs nigh raught unto the ground:
Full large he was of limbe, and shoulders brode,
But of such subtile substance and unsound,
That like a ghost he seem'd, whose grave-clothes were unbound.

XXI
And in his hand a bended bow was seene,
And many arrowes under his right side,
All deadly daungerous, all cruell keene,
Headed with flint, and fethers bloody dide,
Such as the Indians in their quivers hide:
Those could he well direct and streight as line,

And bid them strike the marke which he had eyde;
Ne was there salve, ne was there medicine,
That mote recure their wounds, so inly they did tine.

XXII
As pale and wan as ashes was his looke,
His body leane and meagre as a rake,
And skin all withered like a dryed rooke,
Thereto as cold and drery as a snake,
That seemd to tremble evermore, and quake:
All in a canvas thin he was bedight,
And girded with a belt of twisted brake:
Upon his head he wore an helmet light,
Made of a dead mans skull, that seemd a ghastly sight.

XXIII
Maleger was his name; and after him
There follow'd fast at hand two wicked hags,
With hoary lockes all loose and visage grim;
Their feet unshod, their bodies wrapt in rags,
And both as swift on foot as chased stags;
And yet the one her other legge had lame,
Which with a staffe, all full of litle snags,
She did support, and Impotence her name:
But th' other was Impatience, arm'd with raging flame.

XXIV
Soone as the carle from far the Prince espyde
Glistring in armes and warlike ornament,
His beast he felly prickt on either syde,
And his mischievous bow full readie bent,
With which at him a cruell shaft he sent:
But he was warie, and it warded well
Upon his shield, that it no further went,
But to the ground the idle quarrell fell:
Then he another and another did expell.

XXV
Which to prevent, the Prince his mortall speare
Soone to him raught, and fierce at him did ride,
To be avenged of that shot whyleare:
But he was not so hardy to abide
That bitter stownd, but turning quicke aside
His light-foot beast, fled fast away for feare:
Whom to poursue, the infant after hide,
So fast as his good courser could him beare;
But labour lost it was to weene approch him neare.

XXVI
For as the winged wind his tigre fled,
That vew of eye could scarse him over take,

Ne scarse his feet on ground were seene to tred:
Through hils and dales he speedy way did make,
Ne hedge ne ditch his readie passage brake,
And in his flight the villein turn'd his face,
(As wonts the Tartar by the Caspian lake,
When as the Russian him in fight does chace)
Unto his tygres taile, and shot at him apace.

XXVII
Apace he shot, and yet he fled apace,
Still as the greedy knight nigh to him drew,
And oftentimes he would relent his pace,
That him his foe more fiercely should poursew:
Who when his uncouth manner he did vew,
He gan avize to follow him no more,
But keepe his standing, and his shaftes eschew,
Untill he quite had spent his perlous store,
And then assayle him fresh, ere he could shift for more.

XXVIII
But that lame hag, still as abroad he strew
His wicked arrowes, gathered them againe,
And to him brought, fresh batteill to renew:
Which he espying, cast her to restraine
From yielding succour to that cursed swaine,
And her attaching, thought her hands to tye;
But soone as him dismounted on the plaine
That other hag did far away espye
Binding her sister, she to him ran hastily;

XXIX
And catching hold of him, as downe he lent,
Him backeward overthrew, and downe him stayd
With their rude handes and gryesly graplement,
Till that the villein, comming to their ayd,
Upon him fell, and lode upon him layd:
Full litle wanted, but he had him slaine,
And of the battell balefull end had made,
Had not his gentle squire beheld his paine,
And commen to his reskew, ere his bitter bane.

XXX
So greatest and most glorious thing on ground
May often need the helpe of weaker hand;
So feeble is mans state, and life unsound,
That in assuraunce it may never stand,
Till it dissolved be from earthly band.
Proofe be thou, Prince, the prowest man alyve,
And noblest borne of all in Britayne land;
Yet thee fierce Fortune did so nearely drive,
That had not Grace thee blest, thou shouldest not survive.

XXXI
The squyre arriving, fiercely in his armes
Snatcht first the one, and then the other jade,
His chiefest letts and authors of his harmes,
And them perforce withheld with threatned blade,
Least that his lord they should behinde invade;
The whiles the Prince, prickt with reprochful shame,
As one awakte out of long slombring shade,
Revivyng thought of glory and of fame,
United all his powres to purge him selfe from blame.

XXXII
Like as a fire, the which in hollow cave
Hath long bene underkept and down supprest,
With murmurous disdayne doth inly rave,
And grudge, in so streight prison to be prest,
At last breakes forth with furious unrest,
And strives to mount unto his native seat;
All that did earst it hinder and molest,
Yt now devoures with flames and scorching heat,
And carries into smoake with rage and horror great.

XXXIII
So mightely the Briton Prince him rouzd
Out of his holde, and broke his caytive bands;
And as a beare, whom angry curres have touzd,
Having off-shakt them, and escapt their hands,
Becomes more fell, and all that him with stands
Treads down and overthrowes. Now had the carle
Alighted from his tigre, and his hands
Discharged of his bow and deadly quar'le,
To seize upon his foe flatt lying on the marle.

XXXIV
Which now him turnd to disavantage deare,
For neither can he fly, nor other harme,
But trust unto his strength and manhood meare,
Sith now he is far from his monstrous swarme,
And of his weapons did him selfe disarme.
The knight, yet wrothfull for his late disgrace,
Fiercely advaunst his valorous right arme,
And him so sore smott with his yron mace,
That groveling to the ground he fell, and fild his place.

XXXV
Wel weened hee that field was then his owne,
And all his labor brought to happy end,
When suddein up the villeine overthrowne
Out of his swowne arose, fresh to contend,
And gan him selfe to second battaill bend,

As hurt he had not beene. Thereby there lay
An huge great stone, which stood upon one end,
And had not bene removed many a day;
Some land-marke seemd to bee, or signe of sundry way.

XXXVI
The same he snatcht, and with exceeding sway
Threw at his foe, who was right well aware
To shonne the engin of his meant decay;
It booted not to thinke that throw to beare,
But grownd he gave, and lightly lept areare:
Efte fierce retourning, as a faulcon fayre,
That once hath failed of her souse full neare,
Remounts againe into the open ayre,
And unto better fortune doth her selfe prepayre.

XXXVII
So brave retourning, with his brandisht blade,
He to the carle him selfe agayn addrest,
And strooke at him so sternely, that he made
An open passage through his riven brest,
That halfe the steele behind his backe did rest;
Which drawing backe, he looked ever more
When the hart blood should gush out of his chest,
Or his dead corse should fall upon the flore;
But his dead corse upon the flore fell nathemore.

XXXVIII
Ne drop of blood appeared shed to bee,
All were the wownd so wide and wonderous,
That through his carcas one might playnly see.
Halfe in amaze with horror hideous,
And halfe in rage to be deluded thus,
Again through both the sides he strooke him quight,
That made his spright to grone full piteous:
Yet nathemore forth fled his groning spright,
But freshly as at first, prepard himselfe to fight.

XXXIX
Thereat he smitten was with great affright,
And trembling terror did his hart apall,
Ne wist he what to thinke of that same sight,
Ne what to say, ne what to doe at all;
He doubted least it were some magicall
Illusion, that did beguile his sense,
Or wandring ghost, that wanted funerall,
Or aery spirite under false pretence,
Or hellish feend raysd up through divelish science.

XL
His wonder far exceeded reasons reach,

That he began to doubt his dazeled sight,
And oft of error did him selfe appeach:
Flesh without blood, a person without spright,
Wounds without hurt, a body without might,
That could doe harme, yet could not harmed bee,
That could not die, yet seemd a mortall wight,
That was most strong in most infirmitee;
Like did he never heare, like did he never see.

XLI
A while he stood in this astonishment,
Yet would he not for all his great dismay
Give over to effect his first intent,
And th' utmost meanes of victory assay,
Or th' utmost yssew of his owne decay.
His owne good sword Mordure, that never fayld
At need till now, he lightly threw away,
And his bright shield, that nought him now avayld,
And with his naked hands him forcibly assayld.

XLII
Twixt his two mighty armes him up he snatcht,
And crusht his carcas so against his brest,
That the disdainfull sowle he thence dispatcht,
And th' ydle breath all utterly exprest:
Tho, when he felt him dead, adowne he kest
The lumpish corse unto the sencelesse grownd;
Adowne he kest it with so puissant wrest,
That backe againe it did alofte rebownd,
And gave against his mother Earth a gronefull sownd.

XLIII
As when Joves harnesse-bearing bird from hye
Stoupes at a flying heron with proud disdayne,
The stone-dead quarrey falls so forciblye,
That yt rebownds against the lowly playne,
A second fall redoubling backe agayne.
Then thought the Prince all peril sure was past,
And that he victor onely did remayne;
No sooner thought, then that the carle as fast
Gan heap huge strokes on him, as ere he down was cast.

XLIV
Nigh his wits end then woxe th' amazed knight,
And thought his labor lost and travell vayne,
Against this lifelesse shadow so to fight:
Yet life he saw, and felt his mighty mayne,
That, whiles he marveild still, did still him payne:
Forthy he gan some other wayes advize,
How to take life from that dead-living swayne,
Whom still he marked freshly to arize

From th' earth, and from her womb new spirits to reprize.

XLV
He then remembred well, that had bene sayd,
How th' Earth his mother was, and first him bore;
Shee eke, so often as his life decayd,
Did life with usury to him restore,
And reysd him up much stronger then before,
So soone as he unto her wombe did fall;
Therefore to grownd he would him cast no more,
Ne him committ to grave terrestriall,
But beare him farre from hope of succour usuall.

XLVI
Tho up he caught him twixt his puissant hands,
And having scruzd out of his carrion corse
The lothfull life, now loosd from sinfull hands,
Upon his shoulders carried him perforse
Above three furlongs, taking his full course,
Untill he came unto a standing lake:
Him thereinto he threw without remorse,
Ne stird, till hope of life did him forsake:
So end of that carles dayes, and his owne paynes did make.

XLVII
Which when those wicked hags from far did spye,
Like two mad dogs they ran about the lands;
And th' one of them with dreadfull yelling crye,
Throwing away her broken chaines and bands,
And having quencht her burning fier brands,
Hedlong her selfe did cast into that lake;
But Impotence with her owne wilfull hands
One of Malegers cursed darts did take,
So ryv'd her trembling hart, and wicked end did make.

XLVIII
Thus now alone he conquerour remaines:
Tho, cumming to his squyre, that kept his steed,
Thought to have mounted, but his feeble vaines
Him faild thereto, and served not his need,
Through losse of blood, which from his wounds did bleed,
That he began to faint, and life decay:
But his good squyre, him helping up with speed,
With stedfast hand upon his horse did stay,
And led him to the castle by the beaten way.

XLIX
Where many groomes and squyres ready were
To take him from his steed full tenderly,
And eke the fayrest Alma mett him there
With balme and wine and costly spicery,

To comfort him in his infirmity:
Eftesoones shee causd him up to be convayd,
And of his armes despoyled easily,
In sumptuous bed shee made him to be layd,
And al the while his wounds were dressing, by him stayd.

CANTO XII

Guyon by palmers governaunce
Passing through perilles great,
Doth overthrow the Bowre of Blis,
And Acrasy defeat.

I
Now ginnes this goodly frame of Temperaunce
Fayrely to rise, and her adorned had
To pricke of highest prayse forth to advaunce,
Formerly grounded and fast setteled
On firme foundation of true bountyhed:
And that brave knight, that for this vertue fightes,
Now comes to point of that same perilous sted,
Where Pleasure dwelles in sensuall delights,
Mongst thousand dangers, and ten thousand magick mights.

II
Two dayes now in that sea he sayled has,
Ne ever land beheld, ne living witht,
Ne ought save perill, still as he did pas:
Tho, when appeared the third morrow bright,
Upon the waves to spred her trembling light,
An hideous roring far away they heard,
That all their sences filled with affright,
And streight they saw the raging surges reard
Up to the skyes, that them of drowning made affeard.

III
Said then the boteman, 'Palmer, stere aright,
And keepe an even course; for yonder way
We needes must pas (God doe us well acquight!)
That is the Gulfe of Greedinesse, they say,
That deepe engorgeth all this worldes pray;
Which having swallowd up excessively,
He soone in vomit up againe doth lay,
And belcheth forth his superfluity,
That all the seas for feare doe seeme away to fly.

IV

'On thother syde an hideous rock is pight
Of mightie magnes stone, whose craggie clift
Depending from on high, dreadfull to sight,
Over the waves his rugged armes doth lift,
And threatneth downe to throw his ragged rift
On whoso cometh nigh; yet nigh it drawes
All passengers, that none from it can shift:
For whiles they fly that gulfes devouring jawes,
They on this rock are rent, and sunck in helples wawes.'

V

Forward they passe, and strongly he them rowes,
Untill they nigh unto that gulfe arryve,
Where streame more violent and greedy growes:
Then he with all his puisaunce doth stryve
To strike his oares, and mightily doth dryve
The hollow vessell through the threatfull wave,
Which, gaping wide, to swallow them alyve
In th' huge abysse of his engulfing grave,
Doth rore at them in vaine, and with great terrour rave.

VI

They, passing by, that grisely mouth did see,
Sucking the seas into his entralles deepe,
That seemd more horrible then hell to bee,
Or that darke dreadfull hole of Tartare steepe,
Through which the damned ghosts doen often creep
Backe to the world, bad livers to torment:
But nought that falles into this direfull deepe,
Ne that approcheth nigh the wyde descent,
May backe retourne, but is condemned to be drent.

VII

On thother side they saw that perilous rocke,
Threatning it selfe on them to ruinate,
On whose sharp cliftes the ribs of vessels broke,
And shivered ships, which had beene wrecked late,
Yet stuck, with carcases exanimate
Of such, as having all their substance spent
In wanton joyes and lustes intemperate,
Did afterwardes make shipwrack violent,
Both of their life, and fame for ever fowly blent.

VIII

Forthy this hight the Rock of vile Reproch,
A daungerous and detestable place,
To which nor fish nor fowle did once approch,
But yelling meawes, with seagulles hoars and bace,
And cormoyraunts, with birds of ravenous race,
Which still sat wayting on that wastfull clift
For spoile of wretches, whose unhappy cace,

After lost credit and consumed thrift,
At last them driven hath to this despairefull drift.

IX
The palmer, seeing them in safetie past,
Thus saide: 'Behold th' ensamples in our sightes
Of lustfull luxurie and thriftlesse wast:
What now is left of miserable wightes,
Which spent their looser daies in leud delightes,
But shame and sad reproch, here to be red
By these rent reliques, speaking their ill plightes?
Let all that live, hereby be counselled
To shunne Rock of Reproch, and it as death to dread.'

X
So forth they rowed, and that ferryman
With his stiffe oares did brush the sea so strong,
That the hoare waters from his frigot ran,
And the light bubles daunced all along,
Whiles the salt brine out of the billowes sprong.
At last far off they many islandes spy,
On every side floting the floodes emong:
Then said the knight: 'Lo! I the land descry;
Therefore, old syre, thy course doe thereunto apply.'

XI
'That may not bee,' said then the ferryman,
'Least wee unweeting hap to be fordonne:
For those same islands, seeming now and than,
Are not firme land, nor any certein wonne,
But stragling plots, which to and fro doe ronne
In the wide waters: therefore are they hight
The Wandring Islands. Therefore doe them shonne;
For they have ofte drawne many a wandring wight
Into most deadly daunger and distressed plight.

XII
'Yet well they seeme to him, that farre doth vew,
Both faire and fruitfull, and the grownd dispred
With grassy greene of delectable hew,
And the tall trees with leaves appareled,
Are deckt with blossoms dyde in white and red,
That mote the passengers thereto allure;
But whosoever once hath fastened
His foot thereon, may never it recure,
But wandreth ever more uncertein and unsure.

XIII
'As th' isle of Delos whylome, men report,
Amid th' Aegæan sea long time did stray,
Ne made for shipping any certeine port,

Till that Latona traveiling that way,
Flying from Junoes wrath and hard assay,
Of her fayre twins was there delivered,
Which afterwards did rule the might and day;
Thenceforth it firmely was established,
And for Apolloes honor highly herried.'

XIV
They to him hearken, as beseemeth meete,
And passe on forward: so their way does ly,
That one of those same islands, which doe fleet
In the wide sea, they needes must passen by,
Which seemd so sweet and pleasaunt to the eye,
That it would tempt a man to touchen there:
Upon the banck they sitting did espy
A daintie damsell, dressing of her heare,
By whom a little skippet floting did appeare.

XV
She, them espying, loud to them can call,
Bidding them nigher draw unto the shore;
For she had cause to busie them withall;
And therewith lowdly laught: but nathemore
Would they once turne, but kept on as afore:
Which when she saw, she left her lockes undight,
And running to her boat withouten ore,
From the departing land it launched light,
And after them did drive with all her power and might.

XVI
Whom overtaking, she in merry sort
Them gan to bord, and purpose diversly,
Now faining dalliaunce and wanton sport,
Now throwing forth lewd wordes immodestly;
Till that the palmer gan full bitterly
Her to rebuke, for being loose and light:
Which not abiding, but more scornfully
Scoffing at him that did her justly wite,
She turnd her bote about, and from them rowed quite.

XVII
That was the wanton Phœdria, which late
Did ferry him over the Idle Lake:
Whom nought regarding, they kept on their gate,
And all her vaine allurements did forsake;
When them the wary boteman thus bespake:
'Here now behoveth us well to avyse,
And of our safety good heede to take;
For here before a perlous passage lyes,
Where many mermayds haunt, making false melodies.

XVIII
'But by the way there is a great quick sand,
And a whirlepoole of hidden jeopardy:
Therefore, sir palmer, keepe an even hand;
For twixt them both the narrow way doth ly.'
Scarse had he saide, when hard at hand they spy
That quicksand nigh with water covered;
But by the checked wave they did descry
It plaine, and by the sea discoloured:
It called was the Quickesand of Unthriftyhed.

XIX
They, passing by, a goodly ship did see,
Laden from far with precious merchandize,
And bravely furnished as ship might bee,
Which through great disaventure, or mesprize,
Her selfe had ronne into that hazardize;
Whose mariners and merchants, with much toyle,
Labour'd in vaine to have recur'd their prize,
And the rich wares to save from pitteous spoyle;
But neither toyle nor traveill might her backe recoyle.

XX
On th' other side they see that perilous poole,
That called was the Whirlepoole of Decay,
In which full many had with haplesse doole
Beene suncke, of whom no memorie did stay:
Whose circled waters rapt with whirling sway,
Like to a restlesse wheele, still ronning round,
Did covet, as they passed by that way,
To draw their bote within the utmost bound
Of his wide labyrinth, and then to have them dround.

XXI
But th' heedfull boteman strongly forth did stretch
His brawnie armes, and all his bodie straine,
That th' utmost sandy breach they shortly fetch,
Whiles the dredd daunger does behind remaine.
Suddeine they see from midst of all the maine
The surging waters like a mountaine rise,
And the great sea, puft up with proud disdaine,
To swell above the measure of his guise,
As threatning to devoure all that his powre despise.

XXII
The waves come rolling, and the billowes rore
Outragiously, as they enraged were,
Or wrathfull Neptune did them drive before
His whirling charet, for exceeding feare;
For not one puffe of winde there did appeare;
That all the three thereat woxe much afrayd,

Unweeting what such horrour straunge did reare.
Eftsoones they saw an hideous hoast arrayd
Of huge sea monsters, such as living sence dismayd.

XXIII
Most ugly shapes and horrible aspects,
Such as Dame Nature selfe mote feare to see,
Or shame that ever should so fowle defects
From her most cunning hand escaped bee;
All dreadfull pourtraicts of deformitee:
Spring-headed hydres, and sea-shouldring whales,
Great whirlpooles, which all fishes make to flee,
Bright scolopendraes, arm'd with silver scales,
Mighty monoceros with immeasured tayles,

XXIV
The dreadfull fish, that hath deserv'd the name
Of Death, and like him lookes in dreadfull hew,
The griesly wasserman, that makes his game
The flying ships with swiftnes to pursew,
The horrible sea-satyre, that doth shew
His fearefull face in time of greatest storme,
Huge ziffius, whom mariners eschew
No lesse then rockes, (as travellers informe,)
And greedy rosmarines with visages deforme.

XXV
All these, and thousand thousands many more,
And more deformed monsters thousand fold,
With dreadfull noise and hollow rombling rore,
Came rushing, in the fomy waves enrold,
Which seem'd to fly for feare them to behold:
Ne wonder, if these did the knight appall;
For all, that here on earth we dreadfull hold,
Be but as bugs to fearen babes withall,
Compared to the creatures in the seas entrall.

XXVI
'Feare nought,' then saide the palmer well aviz'd;
'For these same monsters are not these in deed,
But are into these fearefull shapes disguiz'd
By that same wicked witch, to worke us dreed,
And draw from on this journey to proceed.'
Tho, lifting up his vertuous staffe on hye,
He smote the sea, which calmed was with speed,
And all that dreadfull armie fast gan flye
Into great Tethys bosome, where they hidden lye.

XXVII
Quit from that danger, forth their course they kept,
And as they went they heard a ruefull cry

Of one that wayld and pittifully wept,
That through the sea the resounding plaints did fly:
At last they in an island did espy
A seemely maiden, sitting by the shore,
That with great sorrow and sad agony
Seemed some great misfortune to deplore,
And lowd to them for succour called evermore.

XXVIII
Which Guyon hearing, streight his palmer bad
To stere the bote towards that dolefull mayd,
That he might know and ease her sorrow sad:
Who, him avizing better, to him sayd:
'Faire sir, be not displeasd if disobayd:
For ill it were to hearken to her cry;
For she is inly nothing ill apayd,
But onely womanish fine forgery,
Your stubborne hart t' affect with fraile infirmity.

XXIX
'To which when she your courage hath inclind
Through foolish pitty, then her guilefull bayt
She will embosome deeper in your mind,
And for your ruine at the last awayt.'
The knight was ruled, and the boteman strayt
Held on his course with stayed stedfastnesse,
Ne ever shroncke, ne ever sought to bayt
His tyred armes for toylesome wearinesse,
But with his oares did sweepe the watry wildernesse.

XXX
And now they nigh approched to the sted,
Where as those mermayds dwelt: it was a still
And calmy bay, on th' one side sheltered
With the brode shadow of an hoarie hill,
On th' other side an high rocke toured still,
That twixt them both a pleasaunt port they made,
And did like an halfe theatre fulfill:
There those five sisters had continuall trade,
And usd to bath themselves in that deceiptfull shade.

XXXI
They were faire ladies, till they fondly striv'd
With th' Heliconian maides for maystery;
Of whom they over-comen, were depriv'd
Of their proud beautie, and th' one moyity
Transformd to fish, for their bold surquedry;
But th' upper halfe their hew retayned still,
And their sweet skill in wonted melody;
Which ever after they abusd to ill,
T' allure weake traveillers, whom gotten they did kill.

XXXII
So now to Guyon, as he passed by,
Their pleasaunt tunes they sweetly thus applyde:
'O thou fayre sonne of gentle Faery,
That art in mightie armes most magnifyde
Above all knights that ever batteill tryde,
O turne thy rudder hetherward a while:
Here may thy storme-bett vessell safely ryde;
This is the port of rest from troublous toyle,
The worldes sweet in from paine and wearisome turmoyle.'

XXXIII
With that the rolling sea, resounding soft,
In his big base them fitly answered,
And on the rocke the waves breaking aloft,
A solemne meane unto them measured,
The whiles sweet Zephyrus lowd whisteled
His treble, a straunge kinde of harmony;
Which Guyons senses softly tickeled,
That he the boteman bad row easily,
And let him heare some part of their rare melody.

XXXIV
But him the palmer from that vanity
With temperate advice discounselled,
That they it past, and shortly gan descry
The land, to which their course they leveled;
When suddeinly a grosse fog over spred
With his dull vapour all that desert has,
And heavens chearefull face enveloped,
That all things one, and one as nothing was,
And this great universe seemd one confused mas.

XXXV
Thereat they greatly were dismayd, ne wist
How to direct theyr way in darkenes wide,
But feard to wander in that wastefull mist,
For tombling into mischiefe unespide:
Worse is the daunger hidden then descride.
Suddeinly an innumerable flight
Of harmefull fowles, about them fluttering, cride,
And with their wicked wings them ofte did smight,
And sore annoyed, groping in that griesly night.

XXXVI
Even all the nation of unfortunate
And fatall birds about them flocked were,
Such as by nature men abhorre and hate;
The ill-faste owle, deaths dreadfull messengere,
The hoars night-raven, trump of dolefull drere,

The lether-winged batt, dayes enimy,
The ruefull strich, still waiting on the bere,
The whistler shrill, that who so heares doth dy,
The hellish harpyes, prophets of sad destiny.

XXXVII
All those, and all that els does horror breed,
About them flew, and fild their sayles with feare:
Yet stayd they not, but forward did proceed,
Whiles th' one did row, and th' other stifly steare;
Till that at last the weather gan to cleare,
And the faire land it selfe did playnly sheow.
Said then the palmer: 'Lo where does appeare
The sacred soile where all our perills grow;
Therefore, sir knight, your ready arms about you throw.'

XXXVIII
He hearkned, and his armes about him tooke,
The whiles the nimble bote so well her sped,
That with her crooked keele the land she strooke.
Then forth the noble Guyon sallied,
And his sage palmer, that him governed;
But th' other by his bote behind did stay.
They marched fayrly forth, of nought ydred,
Both firmely armd for every hard assay,
With constancy and care, gainst daunger and dismay.

XXXIX
Ere long they heard an hideous bellowing
Of many beasts, that roard outrageously,
As if that hungers poynt or Venus sting
Had them enraged with fell surquedry;
Yet nought they feard, but past on hardily,
Untill they came in vew of those wilde beasts:
Who all attonce, gaping full greedily,
And rearing fercely their upstarting crests,
Ran towards, to devoure those unexpected guests.

XL
But soone as they approcht with deadly threat,
The palmer over them his staffe upheld,
His mighty staffe, that could all charmes defeat:
Eftesoones their stubborne corages were queld,
And high advaunced crests downe meekely feld;
Instead of fraying, they them selves did feare,
And trembled, as them passing they beheld:
Such wondrous powre did in that staffe appeare,
All monsters to subdew to him that did it beare.

XLI
Of that same wood it fram'd was cunningly,

Of which Caduceus whilome was made,
Caduceus, the rod of Mercury,
With which he wonts the Stygian realmes invade,
Through ghastly horror and eternall shade;
Th' infernall feends with it he can asswage,
And Orcus tame, whome nothing can persuade,
And rule the Furyes, when they most doe rage:
Such vertue in his staffe had eke this palmer sage.

XLII
Thence passing forth, they shortly doe arryve
Whereas the Bowre of Blisse was situate;
A place pickt out by choyce of best alyve,
That Natures worke by art can imitate:
In which what ever in this worldly state
Is sweete, and pleasing unto living sense,
Or that may dayntest fantasy aggrate,
Was poured forth with plentifull dispence,
And made there to abound with lavish affluence.

XLIII
Goodly it was enclosed rownd about,
As well their entred guestes to keep within,
As those unruly beasts to hold without;
Yet was the fence thereof but weake and thin;
Nought feard theyr force, that fortilage to win,
But wisedomes powre, and temperaunces might,
By which the mightiest things efforced bin:
And eke the gate was wrought of substaunce light,
Rather for pleasure then for battery or fight.

XLIV
Yt framed was of precious yvory,
That seemd a worke of admirable witt;
And therein all the famous history
Of Jason and Medæa was ywritt;
Her mighty charmes, her furious loving fitt,
His goodly conquest of the golden fleece,
His falsed fayth, and love too lightly flitt,
The wondred Argo, which in venturous peece
First through the Euxine seas bore all the flowr of Greece.

XLV
Ye might have seene the frothy billowes fry
Under the ship, as thorough them she went,
That seemd the waves were into yvory,
Or yvory into the waves were sent;
And otherwhere the snowy substaunce sprent
With vermell, like the boyes blood therein shed,
A piteous spectacle did represent;
And otherwhiles with gold besprinkeled,

Yt seemd thenchaunted flame, which did Creusa wed.

XLVI
All this and more might in that goodly gate
Be red; that ever open stood to all
Which thether came: but in the porch there sate
A comely personage of stature tall,
And semblaunce pleasing, more then naturall,
That traveilers to him seemd to entize;
His looser garment to the ground did fall,
And flew about his heeles in wanton wize,
Not fitt for speedy pace or manly exercize.

XLVII
They in that place him Genius did call:
Not that celestiall powre, to whom the care
Of life, and generation of all
That lives, perteines in charge particulare,
Who wondrous things concerning our welfare,
And straunge phantomes, doth lett us ofte forsee,
And ofte of secret ill bids us beware:
That is our selfe, whom though we doe not see,
Yet each doth in him selfe it well perceive to bee.

XLVIII
Therefore a god him sage antiquity
Did wisely make, and good Agdistes call:
But this same was to that quite contrary,
The foe of life, that good envyes to all,
That secretly doth us procure to fall,
Through guilefull semblants, which he makes us see.
He of this gardin had the governall,
And Pleasures porter was devizd to bee,
Holding a staffe in hand for more formalitee.

XLIX
With diverse flowres he daintily was deckt,
And strowed rownd about, and by his side
A mighty mazer bowle of wine was sett,
As if it had to him bene sacrifide;
Wherewith all new-come guests he gratyfide:
So did he eke Sir Guyon passing by:
But he his ydle curtesie defide,
And overthrew his bowle disdainfully,
And broke his staffe, with which he charmed semblants sly.

L
Thus being entred, they behold arownd
A large and spacious plaine, on every side
Strowed with pleasauns, whose fayre grassy grownd
Mantled with greene, and goodly beautifide

With all the ornaments of Floraes pride,
Wherewith her mother Art, as halfe in scorne
Of niggard Nature, like a pompous bride
Did decke her, and too lavishly adorne,
When forth from virgin bowre she comes in th' early morne.

LI
Thereto the heavens alwayes joviall,
Lookte on them lovely, still in stedfast state,
Ne suffred storme nor frost on them to fall,
Their tender buds or leaves to violate,
Nor scorching heat, nor cold intemperate,
T' afflict the creatures which therein did dwell,
But the milde ayre with season moderate
Gently attempred, and disposd so well,
That still it breathed forth sweet spirit and holesom smell.

LII
More sweet and holesome then the pleasaunt hill
Of Rhodope, on which the nimphe that bore
A gyaunt babe her selfe for griefe did kill;
Or the Thessalian Tempe, where of yore
Fayre Daphne Phæbus hart with love did gore;
Or Ida, where the gods lov'd to repayre,
When ever they their heavenly bowres forlore;
Or sweet Parnasse, the haunt of Muses fayre;
Or Eden selfe, if ought with Eden mote compayre.

LIII
Much wondred Guyon at the fayre aspect
Of that sweet place, yet suffred no delight
To sincke into his sence, nor mind affect,
But passed forth, and lookt still forward right,
Brydling his will, and maystering his might:
Till that he came unto another gate,
No gate, but like one, being goodly dight
With bowes and braunches, which did broad dilate
Their clasping armes, in wanton wreathings intricate:

LIV
So fashioned a porch with rare device,
Archt over head with an embracing vine,
Whose bounches, hanging downe, seemd to entice
All passers by to taste their lushious wine,
And did them selves into their hands incline,
As freely offering to be gathered:
Some deepe empurpled as the hyacine,
Some as the rubine laughing sweetely red,
Some like faire emeraudes, not yet well ripened.

LV

And them amongst, some were of burnisht gold,
So made by art, to beautify the rest,
Which did themselves emongst the leaves enfold,
As lurking from the vew of covetous guest,
That the weake boughes, with so rich load opprest,
Did bow adowne, as overburdened.
Under that porch a comely dame did rest,
Clad in fayre weedes, but fowle disordered,
And garments loose, that seemd unmeet for womanhed.

LVI
In her left hand a cup of gold she held,
And with her right the riper fruit did reach,
Whose sappy liquor, that with fulnesse sweld,
Into her cup she scruzd, with daintie breach
Of her fine fingers, without fowle empeach,
That so faire winepresse made the wine more sweet:
Thereof she usd to give to drinke to each,
Whom passing by she happened to meet:
It was her guise, all straungers goodly so to great.

LVII
So she to Guyon offred it to tast,
Who, taking it out of her tender hond,
The cup to ground did violently cast,
That all in peeces it was broken fond,
And with the liquor stained all the lond:
Whereat Excesse exceedingly was wroth,
Yet no'te the same amend, ne yet with stond,
But suffered him to passe, all were she loth;
Who, nought regarding her displeasure, forward goth.

LVIII
There the most daintie paradise on ground
It selfe doth offer to his sober eye,
In which all pleasures plenteously abownd,
And none does others happinesse envye:
The painted flowres, the trees upshooting hye,
The dales for shade, the hilles for breathing space,
The trembling groves, the christall running by;
And that which all faire workes doth most aggrace,
The art, which all that wrought, appeared in no place.

LIX
One would have thought, (so cunningly the rude
And scorned partes were mingled with the fine,)
That Nature had for wantonesse ensude
Art, and that Art at Nature did repine;
So striving each th' other to undermine,
Each did the others worke more beautify;
So diff'ring both in willes agreed in fine:

So all agreed through sweete diversity,
This gardin to adorne with all variety.

LX
And in the midst of all a fountaine stood,
Of richest substance that on earth might bee,
So pure and shiny that the silver flood
Through every channell running one might see:
Most goodly it with curious ymageree
Was overwrought, and shapes of naked boyes,
Of which some seemd with lively jollitee
To fly about playing their wanton toyes,
Whylest others did them selves embay in liquid joyes.

LXI
And over all, of purest gold was spred
A trayle of yvie in his native hew:
For the rich metall was so coloured,
That wight, who did not well avis'd it vew,
Would surely deeme it to bee yvie trew:
Low his lascivious armes adown did creepe,
That themselves dipping in the silver dew,
Their fleecy flowres they tenderly did steepe,
Which drops of christall seemd for wantones to weep.

LXII
Infinit streames continually did well
Out of this fountaine, sweet and faire to see,
The which into an ample laver fell,
And shortly grew to so great quantitie,
That like a litle lake it seemd to bee;
Whose depth exceeded not three cubits hight,
That through the waves one might the bottom see,
All pav'd beneath with jaspar shining bright,
That seemd the fountaine in that sea did sayle upright.

LXIII
And all the margent round about was sett
With shady laurell trees, thence to defend
The sunny beames, which on the billowes bett,
And those which therein bathed mote offend.
As Guyon hapned by the same to wend,
Two naked damzelles he therein espyde,
Which, therein bathing, seemed to contend
And wrestle wantonly, ne car'd to hyde
Their dainty partes from vew of any which them eyd.

LXIV
Sometimes the one would lift the other quight
Above the waters, and then downe againe
Her plong, as over maystered by might,

Where both awhile would covered remaine,
And each the other from to rise restraine;
The whiles their snowy limbes, as through a vele,
So through the christall waves appeared plaine:
Then suddeinly both would themselves unhele,
And th' amarous sweet spoiles to greedy eyes revele.

LXV
As that faire starre, the messenger of morne,
His deawy face out of the sea doth reare,
Or as the Cyprian goddesse, newly borne
Of th' oceans fruitfull froth, did first appeare,
Such seemed they, and so their yellow heare
Christalline humor dropped downe apace.
Whom such when Guyon saw, he drew him neare,
And somewhat gan relent his earnest pace;
His stubborne brest gan secret pleasaunce to embrace.

LXVI
The wanton maidens, him espying, stood
Gazing a while at his unwonted guise;
Then th' one her selfe low ducked in the flood,
Abasht that her a straunger did avise:
But thother rather higher did arise,
And her two lilly paps aloft displayd,
And all, that might his melting hart entyse
To her delights, she unto him bewrayd:
The rest, hidd underneath, him more desirous made.

LXVII
With that the other likewise up arose,
And her faire lockes, which formerly were bownd
Up in one knott, she low adowne did lose:
Which, flowing long and thick, her cloth'd arownd,
And th'yvorie in golden mantle gownd:
So that faire spectacle from him was reft,
Yet that which reft it no lesse faire was fownd:
So hidd in lockes and waves from lookers theft,
Nought but her lovely face she for his looking left.

LXVIII
Withall she laughed, and she blusht withall,
That blushing to her laughter gave more grace,
And laughter to her blushing, as did fall.
Now when they spyde the knight to slacke his pace,
Them to behold, and in his sparkling face
The secrete signes of kindled lust appeare,
Their wanton meriments they did encrease,
And to him beckned to approch more neare,
And shewd him many sights, that corage cold could reare.

LXIX
On which when gazing him the palmer saw,
He much rebukt those wandring eyes of his,
And, counseld well, him forward thence did draw.
Now are they come nigh to the Bowre of Blis,
Of her fond favorites so nam'd amis:
When thus the palmer: 'Now, sir, well avise;
For here the end of all our traveill is:
Here wonnes Acrasia, whom we must surprise,
Els she will slip away, and all our drift despise.'

LXX
Eftsoones they heard a most melodious sound,
Of all that mote delight a daintie eare,
Such as attonce might not on living ground,
Save in this paradise, be heard elswhere:
Right hard it was for wight which did it heare,
To read what manner musicke that mote bee:
For all that pleasing is to living eare
Was there consorted in one harmonee;
Birdes, voices, instruments, windes, waters, all agree.

LXXI
The joyous birdes, shrouded in chearefull shade,
Their notes unto the voice attempred sweet:
Th' angelicall soft trembling voyces made
To th' instruments divine respondence meet:
The silver sounding instruments did meet
With the base murmure of the waters fall
The waters fall with difference discreet,
Now soft, now loud, unto the wind did call:
The gentle warbling wind low answered to all.

LXXII
There, whence that musick seemed heard to bee,
Was the faire witch, her selfe now solacing
With a new lover, whom, through sorceree
And witchcraft, she from farre did thether bring:
There she had him now laid a slombering,
In secret shade after long wanton joyes:
Whilst round about them pleasauntly did sing
Many faire ladies and lascivious boyes,
That ever mixt their song with light licentious toyes.

Shames her in her sexual relations

LXXIII
And all that while, right over him she hong,
With her false eyes fast fixed in his sight,
As seeking medicine whence she was stong,
Or greedily depasturing delight:
And oft inclining downe, with kisses light,
For feare of waking him, his lips bedewd,

She holds the power in this situation

And through his humid eyes did sucke his spright,
Quite molten into lust and pleasure lewd;
Wherewith she sighed soft, as if his case she rewd.

LXXIV
The whiles some one did chaunt this lovely lay:—
Ah! see, who so fayre thing doest faine to see,
In springing flowre the image of thy day;
Ah! see the virgin rose, how sweetly shee
Doth first peepe foorth with bashfull modestee,
That fairer seemes, the lesse ye see her may;
Lo! see soone after, how more bold and free
Her bared bosome she doth broad display;
Lo! see soone after, how she fades and falls away.

LXXV
So passeth, in the passing of a day,
Of mortall life the leafe, the bud, the flowre,
Ne more doth florish after first decay,
That earst was sought to deck both bed and bowre
Of many a lady, and many a paramowre:
Gather therefore the rose, whilest yet is prime,
For soone comes age, that will her pride deflowre:
Gather the rose of love, whilest yet is time,
Whilest loving thou mayst loved be with equall crime.

LXXVI
He ceast, and then gan all the quire of birdes
Their diverse notes t' attune unto his lay,
As in approvaunce of his pleasing wordes.
The constant payre heard all that he did say,
Yet swarved not, but kept their forward way,
Through many covert groves and thickets close,
In which they creeping did at last display
That wanton lady, with her lover lose,
Whose sleepie head she in her lap did soft dispose.

LXXVII
Upon a bed of roses she was layd,
As faint through heat, or dight to pleasant sin,
And was arayd, or rather disarayd,
All in a vele of silke and silver thin,
That hid no whit her alablaster skin,
But rather shewd more white, if more might bee:
More subtile web Arachne cannot spin,
Nor the fine nets, which oft we woven see
Of scorched deaw, do not in th' ayre more lightly flee.

LXXVIII
Her snowy brest was bare to ready spoyle
Of hungry eies, which n'ote therewith be fild;

And yet through languour of her late sweet toyle,
Few drops, more cleare then nectar, forth distild,
That like pure orient perles adowne it trild;
==And her faire eyes, sweet smyling in delight,==
==Moystened their fierie beames, with which she thrild==
Fraile harts, yet quenched not, like starry light,
Which, sparckling on the silent waves, does seeme more bright.

LXXIX

The young man, sleeping by her, seemd to be
Some goodly swayne of honorable place,
That certes it great pitty was to see
Him his nobility so fowle deface:
A sweet regard and amiable grace,
Mixed with manly sternesse, did appeare,
Yet sleeping, in his well proportioned face,
And on his tender lips the downy heare
Did now but freshly spring, and silken blossoms beare.

LXXX

His warlike armes, the ydle instruments
Of sleeping praise, were hong upon a tree,
And his brave shield, full of old moniments,
Was fowly ra'st, that none the signes might see;
Ne for them, ne for honour, cared hee,
Ne ought that did to his advauncement tend,
But in lewd loves, and wastfull luxuree,
His dayes, his goods, his bodie he did spend:
O horrible enchantment, that him so did blend!

LXXXI

The noble Elfe and carefull palmer drew
So nigh them, minding nought but lustfull game,
That suddein forth they on them rusht, and threw
A subtile net, which only for that same
The skilfull palmer formally did frame:
So held them under fast, the whiles the rest
Fled all away for feare of fowler shame.
The faire enchauntresse, so unwares opprest,
Tryde all her arts and all her sleights, thence out to wrest.

LXXXII

And eke her lover strove: but all in vaine;
For that same net so cunningly was wound,
That neither guile nor force might it distraine.
They tooke them both, and both them strongly bound
In captive bandes, which there they readie found:
But her in chaines of adamant he tyde;
For nothing else might keepe her safe and sound;
But Verdant (so he hight) he soone untyde,
And counsell sage in steed thereof to him applyde.

LXXXIII
But all those pleasaunt bowres and pallace brave
Guyon broke downe, with rigour pittilesse;
Ne ought their goodly workmanship might save
Them from the tempest of his wrathfulnesse,
But that their blisse he turn'd to balefulnesse:
Their groves he feld, their gardins did deface,
Their arbers spoyle, their cabinets suppresse,
Their banket houses burne, their buildings race,
And, of the fayrest late, now made the fowlest place.

LXXXIV
Then led they her away, and eke that knight
They with them led, both sorrowfull and sad:
The way they came, the same retourn'd they right,
Till they arrived where they lately had
Charm'd those wild-beasts, that rag'd with furie mad:
Which, now awaking, fierce at them gan fly,
As in their mistresse reskew, whom they lad;
But them the palmer soone did pacify.
Then Guyon askt, what meant those beastes which there did ly.

LXXXV
Sayd he: 'These seeming beasts are men indeed,
Whom this enchauntresse hath transformed thus,
Whylome her lovers, which her lustes did feed,
Now turned into figures hideous,
According to their mindes like monstruous.'
'Sad end,' quoth he, 'of life intemperate,
And mournefull meed of joyes delicious!
But, palmer, if it mote thee so aggrate,
Let them returned be unto their former state.'

LXXXVI
Streight way he with his vertuous staffe them strooke,
And streight of beastes they comely men became;
Yet being men they did unmanly looke,
And stared ghastly, some for inward shame,
And some for wrath, to see their captive dame:
But one above the rest in speciall,
That had an hog beene late, hight Grylle by name,
Repyned greatly, and did him miscall,
That had from hoggish forme him brought to naturall.

LXXXVII
Saide Guyon: 'See the mind of beastly man,
That hath so soone forgot the excellence
Of his creation, when he life began,
That now he chooseth, with vile difference,
To be a beast, and lacke intelligence.'

To whom the palmer thus: 'The donghill kinde
Delightes in filth and fowle incontinence:
Let Gryll be Gryll, and have his hoggish minde;
But let us hence depart, whilest wether serves and winde.'

Edmund Spenser – A Short Biography

One of the greatest of English poets, Edmund Spenser was born in East Smithfield, London, in 1552, though an exact date is not recorded.

As a boy, he was educated in London at the Merchant Taylors' School and later at Pembroke College, Cambridge.

As a young man, in 1578, the young Edmund was, for a short time, secretary to John Young, the Bishop of Rochester.

In 1579, he published The Shepheardes Calender, his first major work. The poem follows Colin Clout, a folk character originated by John Skelton, and depicts his life as a shepherd through the twelve months of the year.

It is also around this time that Edmund was married for the first time to Machabyas Childe. The union produced two children; Sylvanus and Katherine.

Edmund journeyed to Ireland in July 1580, in the service of the newly appointed Lord Deputy, Arthur Grey, 14th Baron Grey de Wilton. His time included the terrible massacre at the Siege of Smerwick, though this event seems to have settled his views somewhat on Ireland and the Irish. (The Siege of Smerwick took place at Ard na Caithne in 1580, during the Second Desmond Rebellion. A 400–500 strong force of Papal soldiers captured the town but were later forced to retreat to nearby Dún an Óir, where they were besieged by the English Army and eventually surrendered. On the orders of the English Commander most were then massacred).

When Lord Grey was recalled to England, Edmund stayed, having being appointed to several other official posts and lands in the Munster Plantation. Between 1587 and 1589, Spenser acquired his main estate at Kilcolman, near Doneraile in North Cork.

He later bought a second holding to the south, at Rennie, on a rock overlooking the river Blackwater but still in North Cork. Its ruins are still visible today. A short distance away grew a tree, locally known as "Spenser's Oak". Local legend has it that he penned some of The Faerie Queene under this very tree.

This epic poem, The Faerie Queene, is acknowledged as Edmund's masterpiece. The first three books were published in 1590, and a second set of three books were published in 1596. The original idea was for the poem to consist of twelve books. So although the version we publish here is all that he actually wrote it is still one of the longest, and most magnificent, poems in English literature.

The Faerie Queene is a work on several levels of allegory, including as praise of Queen Elizabeth I. The poem follows several knights in an examination of several virtues. In Spenser's "A Letter of the Authors," he states that the entire epic poem is "cloudily enwrapped in allegorical devises," and that the aim behind The Faerie Queene was to "fashion a gentleman or noble person in virtuous and gentle discipline."

On its publication Spenser travelled to London to publish and promote the work. In this endeavour he was successful enough to obtain a life pension of £50 a year from the Queen who did not give these out lightly.

Spenser used a verse form, now called the Spenserian stanza, in The Faerie Queene as well as several others poems. The stanza's main meter is iambic pentameter with a final line in iambic hexameter (having six stresses, known as an Alexandrine). He was also to use his own rhyme scheme for the sonnet. In a Spenserian sonnet, the last line of every stanza is linked with the first line of the next one.

Spenser was well read in classical literature and strove to emulate such Roman poets as Virgil and Ovid, whom he had studied during his schooling.

Indeed the reality is that Spenser, through his great talents, was able to move Poetry in a different direction. It led to him being called a Poet's Poet and brought rich admiration from Milton, Raleigh, Blake, Wordsworth, Keats, Byron, and Lord Tennyson, among others. John Milton in his Areopagitica called Spenser "our sage and serious poet . . . whom I dare be known to think a better teacher than Scotus or Aquinas".

He had hoped this praise and pension might lead to a position at Court but his next work antagonised the queen's principal secretary, Lord Burghley, through the inclusion of the satirical Mother Hubberd's Tale.

Spenser returned to Ireland and in 1591, Complaints, a collection of poems that voices complaints in mournful or mocking tones was published.

By 1594, Spenser's first wife, Machabyas, had died. Very soon he married Elizabeth Boyle, and to which he dedicated the sonnet sequence Amoretti. The marriage itself was celebrated in Epithalamion and the fruit of this relationship was a son, Peregrine.

In 1595, Spenser now published Amoretti and Epithalamion. The volume contains eighty-nine sonnets.

In the following year Spenser released Prothalamion, a wedding song written for the daughters of a duke, allegedly in hopes to gain favour in the court. More importantly he also wrote a prose pamphlet titled A View of the Present State of Ireland (A Veue of the Present State of Irelande). It was circulated in manuscript form due to its highly inflammatory content. Its main argument was that Ireland would never be totally 'pacified' by the English until its indigenous language and customs had been destroyed, if necessary by violence.

Spenser was a strong proponent of, and wished devoutly, that the Irish language should be eradicated, writing that if children learn Irish before English, "Soe that the speach being Irish, the hart must needes be Irishe; for out of the aboundance of the hart, the tonge speaketh".

He further discussed in the pamphlet future draconian plans to subjugate Ireland, after the most recent rising, led by Hugh O'Neill, having again shown the failure of previous efforts. The work is also a partial defence of Lord Arthur Grey de Wilton, with whom Spenser previously served and who deeply influenced Spenser's views on Ireland.

The goal of this piece was to show that Ireland was in great need of reform. Spenser believed that "Ireland is a diseased portion of the State, it must first be cured and reformed, before it could be in a position to appreciate the good sound laws and blessings of the nation". Spenser categorises the "evils" of the Irish people into three distinct categories: laws, customs, and religion. These three elements work together in creating the disruptive and degraded people. One example given in the work is the native law system called "Brehon Law" which trumps the established law given by the English monarchy. This system has its own court and way of dealing with troubles. It has been passed down through the generations and Spenser views this system as a native and backward custom which must be destroyed. (As an example the Brehon Law methods of dealing with murder by imposing an éraic, or fine, on the murderer's whole family particularly horrified the English, in whose Protestant view a murderer should die for his act.)

He pressed for a scorched earth policy in Ireland, noting that the destruction of crops and animals had been successful in crushing the Second Desmond Rebellion of which he was a part.

However in 1598, during the Nine Years War, Spenser was, ironically, driven from his home by the native Irish forces of Aodh Ó Néill. His castle at Kilcolman was burned.

In 1599, Spenser travelled to London, where he died on January 13th at the age of forty-six. According to Ben Jonson, in another and tragic irony it was "for want of bread".

Edmund Spenser's coffin was carried to his grave in Westminster Abbey by other poets, who threw many pens and pieces of poetry into his grave followed with many tears.

His second wife, Elizabeth, survived him and went on to remarry twice.

Spenser was called a Poets' Poet and was admired by John Milton, William Blake, William Wordsworth, John Keats, Lord Byron, and Alfred Lord Tennyson, among others. Walter Raleigh wrote a dedicatory poem to The Faerie Queene in 1590, in which he claims to admire and value Spenser's work more so than any other in the English language. John Milton in his Areopagitica called Spenser "our sage and serious poet . . . whom I dare be known to think a better teacher than Scotus or Aquinas".

It is praise indeed and clearly shows why Edmund Spenser is indeed part of the Pantheon of our greatest Poets.

Edmund Spenser – A Concise Bibliography

1569 - Jan van der Noodt's A theatre for Worldlings, including poems translated into English by Spenser from French sources.

1579 - The Shepheardes Calender, published under the pseudonym "Immerito".

1580 - Three proper, and wittie, familar letters

1590 - The Faerie Queene, Books I–III

1591 - Complaints, Containing sundrie small Poemes of the Worlds Vanitie

1592 - Axiochus, a translation of a pseudo-Platonic dialogue from the original Ancient Greek; attributed to "Edw: Spenser" but the attribution is uncertain

1592 - Daphnaïda. An Elegy upon the death of the noble and vertuous Douglas Howard, Daughter and heire of Henry Lord Howard, Viscount Byndon, and wife of Arthure Gorges Esquier

1595 - Amoretti and Epithalamion

1595 - Astrophel. A Pastorall Elegie vpon the death of the most Noble and valorous Knight, Sir Philip Sidney.

1595 - Colin Clouts Come home againe

1596 - Four Hymns (poem)|Fowre Hymnes dedicated from the court at Greenwich.

1596 - Prothalamion

1596 - The Faerie Queene, Books IV-VI

1598 - A Veue of the Present State of Irelande (Manuscript)

1599 - Babel, Empress of the East – a dedicatory poem prefaced to Lewes Lewkenor's The Commonwealth of Venice.

1609 - Two Cantos of Mutabilitie published together with a reprint of The Fairie Queene.

1611 - First folio edition of Spenser's collected works

1633 - A Veue of the Present State of Irelande, a prose treatise on the reformation of Ireland.